WORKED EXAMPLES

ECONOMICS BOOK ONE

by

A. Stephen

CELTIC REVISION AIDS

CELTIC REVISION AIDS
Lincoln Way, Windmill Road,
Sunbury on Thames, Middlesex

First published in this edition 1979

ISBN 017 751159 1

Printed in Hong Kong

INTRODUCTION

This book is not a set of model answers to be learnt and repeated at the examination. It is an attempt to show the A level candidate how he might tackle the sort of questions that appear on A level papers. Many of the questions are taken from past papers.

I am grateful to the following examination boards for permission to reproduce questions from their A Level Economics papers.

The Boards, of course, accept no responsibility for the suggested answers given.
University Entrance and School Examinations Council of the University of London.
The Associated Examining Board.
The Joint Matriculation Board.
University of Cambridge Local Examinations Syndicate.
Oxford Delegacy of Local Examinations.
Southern Universities Joint Board for School Examinations.
Welsh Joint Examination Committee.

CONTENTS

1. How far do you consider the definition of economic theory as "the logic of choice" to be adequate?

Economics is a comparatively young subject and has been defined in a number of ways. Some definitions are conflicting and some are complementary. No common, generally accepted definition yet prevails but increasingly agreement is centering around definitions which deal with choice.

The word "economics" is probably derived partly from the Greek word "oikonomia", meaning household management. This led people to believe that economics was the study of how to be economical. However, economics does not set out to tell people what to do, but it is an analytical study telling people what would happen, should they follow some particular course. It certainly makes no moral judgements and has no connection with ethics. Thus, any definition of economics suggesting that it shows people how to be economical or any definition attempting a moral judgement is not a good definition of economics.

Some economists have approached economics in the light of the fact that most things in this world are scarce and that people are continually – whether they realise it or not – making choices and deciding what they shall do, which they will choose and so on. Some things, of course, are not scarce and so do not come into the realm of economic theory – air, water, sunshine and such things are used by everybody at any time, and people cannot determine their supply. Whether they are demanded or not, they will still be there. Thus economics is concerned with those things which are scarce – but things may only be scarce in relation to demand and hence any definition of economics should include in its range, the supply and demand of scarce goods.

Definitions of economics should also include, directly or by implication, some reference to distribution and exchange. Goods are produced partially so that they may be exchanged against other goods. Economic theory, therefore, ought to cover production, consumption, exchange, distribution and public finance.

What happens to the definition of economics as "the logic of choice" in this light? Every individual is making some choice which affects the economic system. A man who chooses to become a decorator instead of a carpenter is exerting some influence on the economic system. It is the sum of these individual choices that is important rather than individual choices themselves. If all rising young carpenters suddenly decided to become decorators that would greatly affect the economic system. Economics is concerned with choices and the sum of choices. Whether a person has three baths a week or four has some economic effect in the long run.

"In the long run" is an important concept in itself. A person's decision rarely has an *immediate* effect and, at the time that it is made, will be of absolutely no significance at all. Hence "logic" is quite an important part of a definition concerned with choices. The logical implications of the choice are important and not so much the fact that the choice has been made. It is what will happen in the long run that matters. Referring again to the person who chooses between three and four baths a week, its economic significance is not apparent immediately but only in the fullness of time.

Clearly not all choices have economic significance. For example, the choice of moves in a game of chess has no bearing on economics. It could therefore be argued that to define economic theory as "the logic of choice" is too far-reaching. It should be noted that there are some important facts which have economic significance but yet about which there is no choice. The stock of coal underground has economic significance and yet there can be no choice about it. Perhaps in the end we settle therefore for Robbins' definition as "a study of the relationship between ends and scarce means which have alternative uses."

2. What do you understand by the term "opportunity cost"? How is it related to the problem of scarcity? (L)

Economics can be thought of as attempting to tackle the problem of the allocation of scarce resources. To the economist, the word scarcity relates to any resource the supply of which is short of infinite. There is no single good the supply of which is infinite, and therefore a choice has to be made between goods.

The consumer, in this situation, cannot have everything that he wants and has therefore to order or rank his preferences. In practice his ability to purchase goods depends on his income, but subconsciously he will still find himself ranking his preferences and will find that he will have to trade-off one type of good for another. For example he may find that he has spent all his money for a week except for 60p, having paid for food, rent, heating, lighting, clothes, H.P. and so on. The choice before him may be that he can make one visit to the cinema or go to a pub and have a couple of pints of beer. He cannot have both. Having got to this point it should be noted that the food, rent, etc. all come higher in his list of priorities than the marginal visit to the cinema or the pub, but at this margin a choice has to be made. Let it be assumed that he chooses to go to a pub in which case the cost (i.e. the loss) is equivalent to the visit to the pictures which in the consumer's opinion was the next best alternative use of his money. Economists describe this as the opportunity cost. It can thus be defined as "the cost of using something in a particular venture is the benefit foregone (opportunity cost) by not using it in its best alternative use." The principle of opportunity cost applies to all goods because, in principle, money can always be spent in an alternative way. The individual therefore is assumed to have a set of preferences all of which follow one another very closely. The opportunity cost of spending money on one good is therefore equivalent to the loss of utility that would have been derived from the next good in the list of preferences.

The principle of opportunity cost applies not only to individual consumers but also to governments which also have income constraints and a substantial variety of projects on which they can spend money. Thus a government having settled top priority tasks may have some money which it can, let us assume, spend on building a number of new hospitals or the purchase of a new aircraft carrier. If it chooses one, the cost of that choice is equivalent to the loss of ability that would have been derived from having the other.

There are a number of important applications of this principle. For example firms when costing how much a particular project will cost may not include any cost of "borrowing" money if that money comes from profits made the previous year. This is a fundamental error because though having this money means the firm does not have to pay someone else, the money still has an opportunity cost because it can be used to lend to someone else. Earlier, opportunity cost was considered in terms of the next best alternative. In this case the firm would have at least been able to lend the money to a building society and their rate of interest has been foregone if the money is used for an "internal" project, and it is therefore reasonable to charge the project with these costs.

The principles behind opportunity cost also have applications in the field of social economics. A government might be considering the closure of a coal mine staffed largely by relatively old miners who could find no alternative employment. These miners, if the mine closed, might all draw social security benefits. The opportunity cost is high because the next best alternative to keeping the mine open is no production with all miners drawing social security. The government, after considering the opportunity cost, might feel it would be cheaper to keep the mine open.

The concept is frequently applied in explanations of international trade.

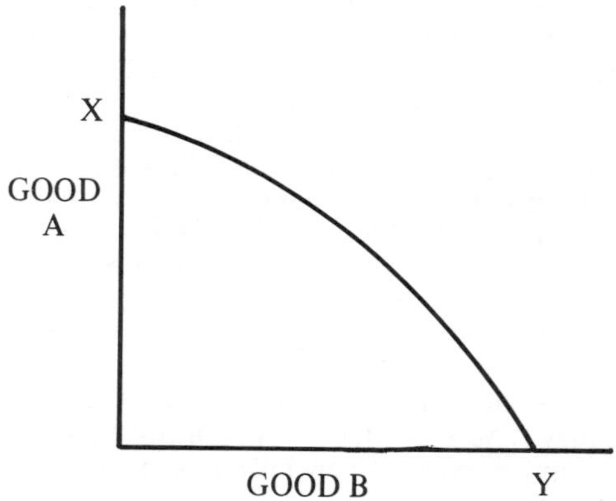

In the diagram above it is assumed that two goods are produced in a national economy determined by the line XY. This line illustrates that if more of Good A is produced then less of Good B will be produced. The opportunity cost of B can therefore be thought of as the amount of A that has to be foregone to produce it. It is often suggested that trade between countries takes place where the opportunity costs of production of goods differ.

3. "The costs of economic growth are greater than the benefits." Discuss. (L)

During the 1960's it was the declared objective of successive Labour and Conservative Governments to increase the rate of growth. Growth here was defined in terms of increasing the Gross National Product per head. There were, of course, other objectives pursued by such governments and at times of balance of payments difficulties or high unemployment then the maximisation of growth objective was put temporarily in abeyance. But in general the pursuance of a high level of economic growth was thought to be desirable, in part because it had eluded Britain in the years since 1945.

The benefits of growth were thought to barely need exposition. A growth in GNP meant that more people had more goods and services which would, in turn, make them happier. It was also thought that a higher level of GNP meant that more money could be spent on social programmes, education and foreign aid. It was thought that improving the standard of living of the nation was important, in part because other countries in Europe were growing faster. For example growth rate in the U.K. 1950-64 was only 2.2% compared to that of 3.7% in France and 5.1% in West Germany. It was argued that benefits of growth over time were apparent to all in terms of better quality food, housing, health.

By the end of the 1960's however there was a very powerful anti-growth lobby both in Europe and America. This lobby argued that growth was not a desirable objective, and that if growth rates continued as at present then man would no longer be able to support himself on this planet. The most powerful documented case prepared for this point of view is by Professor D. Meadows and called "Limits to Growth". It is a giant computer program/mathematical model which extrapolates present trends beyond the year 2000 to examine the implications for mankind. It isolates two important causes of potential disaster one of which is pollution and the other is the destruction of irreplaceable raw materials. Even the most optimistic assumptions about slowing down of rates of usage of such materials, or build up of pollution resulted in a marked worsening of man's environment in the period after the 1980's. Meadows therefore christened the present period a "Golden Age" in which the environment was still tolerable and which also was able to pursue policies designed to yield a high material standard of living.

It would not be wholly correct to assume that this point of view has been totally accepted. Much work is being carried out on the verification of the Meadows model and various criticisms have been made of it. Nevertheless there has been a distinct swing in public and government opinion away from the previous uncritical acceptance of the goal of economic growth and a more critical appreciation of the benefits of growth is apparent. For example there can be little doubt that some countries have increased their rate of economic growth and at the same time increased the levels of pollution. It is also accepted that growth rate will slow if money is spent on reducing pollution – such as fitting after-burners to vehicles, or controlling effluent put into rivers. Nevertheless it is still argued that growth should be pursued as an objective in order to provide money to pay for the better environment. It is also more accepted that growth should be in pollution-free industries and that industries have a duty to protect the environment.

Another unfortunate by-product of growth is the damage it does to the landscape in the building of roads. There is little doubt that a good system of communications is essential to a rapidly growing economy and this means that new roads have to be built. Sometimes such roads fundamentally change the character of areas of outstanding natural beauty – such as the M.40 at Stokenchurch. Sometimes roads destroy urban environments resulting in large numbers of people having to move house and others having to live next to noisy roads – e.g. London's West Way. Government policy in these matters no longer shows the callousness of previous eras by assuming that some people were bound to suffer in the name of progress. Much greater consultation and co-operation is apparent and recently the Department of the Environment accepted the principle that objectors could object not only to the siting of a road but could question the need for the road in the first place.

A third- by-product of rapid economic growth is the exhaustion of raw materials. For a number of years concern has been voiced over the possibility of shortage of oil and petroleum and this has been increased recently by the action of the OPEC group in restricting output of oil. Concern has also been expressed over possible shortages of other raw materials notably the more important metals. Finally with the rapid rate of industrialisation and urbanisation as well as rapid population growth, serious fears have been expressed whether man is likely to have a sufficiently active agriculture to feed himself. The ghost of Malthus has risen again!

Some of this may appear outside the sphere of economics but the task of the economist is to allocate scarce resources. It has been assumed that the consumer has the choice and that such problems are solved by the operation of market forces. But such authorities as E. H. Mishan have questioned whether the consumer is sovereign. He may be better fed, better clothed but is he necessarily happier in a noisy, smelly world where the incidence of mental disorder is high, in part due to the pressures of modern life?

There are then powerful arguments against economic growth. Nevertheless few people would deny that some growth is necessary but most would agree that such growth should make full use of re-cycled materials, produce minimum effluent and should destroy as little of the natural environment as possible. The formulation of a policy to achieve such objectives however, is extremely difficult.

4. Distinguish between prime costs and overhead costs. Explain with examples the economic importance of these distinctions. (A.E.B.)

Some costs vary directly with output. The costs of most raw materials, labour and – to a certain degree – power and lighting are large when output is large and fall as output falls. These are variable costs, the specific costs incurred in the production of a commodity, which vary with the amount produced. These costs, together with certain fixed costs (e.g. salaries of administrative staff) which must be covered if any production is to take place, constitute prime costs.

Other costs involved in production do not vary as output varies. Rent, rates, debenture interest and so on have to be incurred whether production is taking place fully or not. These are fixed costs and do not vary with output. Such fixed costs are known as supplementary or overhead costs which must be covered in the long run.

If overhead costs form a large proportion of total costs, a business man is reluctant to leave the market when prices are falling, because he can do so only at the risk of incurring considerable financial loss. He may, in a period of difficulty, be prepared to sell for a time at a price that does not cover his total costs, if by so doing he can cover his prime costs. Unless he ceases production completely, his overhead costs will continue at a constant level irrespective of whether much or little is produced. If the price that can be obtained covers prime costs and, if possible, makes some contribution to overhead costs, it may pay the business man to continue to produce rather than to close down. He cannot continue to produce at a price below total costs indefinitely, but he may do so for a considerable time if there is a possibility that conditions will improve or if he can expect to achieve some economies that will reduce total costs. If the situation becomes hopeless, he will have to go out of production. In any event, he will stop producing when he is certain that his overhead costs cannot be covered in the long run.

If the costs involved include charges for interest on his own capital and rent on his own land and buildings, he need not pay those items in cash and so can extend the period during which he can continue to produce at a price below total costs. Likewise, he may neglect to provide for depreciation on his plant and machinery, but he can only do this for a limited time or he will find that his plant has worn out and he will have no funds with which to replace it.

When prime costs form the main part of total costs and overhead costs are comparatively small, production may cease as soon as price falls below total costs, for in such a case most of the costs increase with output. In coal-mining, for instance, prime costs constitute a large element of total costs, the wages bill being a substantial part.

The costs of running a railway, on the other hand, are largely overhead costs. The track, the trains and most of the staff exist whether one train or one hundred trains are run and whether it travels ten miles or a hundred miles.

5. What do you understand by Cost Benefit Analysis? (L)

In private industry decisions regarding level of investment are taken on the basis of the most profitable use of funds. Profit is assumed to be the objective and any investment scheme which is thought to yield a satisfactory level of profit will be acceptable.

In the public sector, however, the objectives of policy are not usually the maximisation of profit. Frequently they are a combination of providing services at moderate cost, minimising environmental disruption or disturbance, yet using resources as efficiently as possible. There is therefore no single objective but a number of frequently conflicting goals which have to be pursued by the public decision-taker.

Cost benefit analysis is used to compare these conflicting goals so that, hopefully, the decision-maker will have the issues before him clarified, thus enabling him to make a more rational decision. The contexts in which cost benefit analysis have been used include most areas of public life, such as the evaluation of proposals to build a new motorway, the analysis of government research and development, and even the comparison of different national defence systems (though here the term "cost-effectiveness" is used as the objectives are set and the aim is to determine that system which is the cheapest way of satisfying such objectives).

Probably the most famous cost benefit analysis was the Roskill Commission on the Third London Airport. Unlike the case of national defence the objectives of the study were not easy to identify. The commission had to consider the wishes of, and the implications for, a number of groups of people e.g. the airlines, airline passengers, those who lived in or around the sites for the proposed airfield, and the environmental impact of any choice.

Cost benefit analysis makes various assumptions, then tries to quantify the implications for each affected group. In order to illustrate the technique it is probably easiest to take the evaluation procedure carried out for new roads or road improvement schemes by the Department of the Environment. Here the costs of the scheme are relatively easy to determine being the costs of building the road. The benefits of the scheme are divided between three groups. Firstly, time savings to existing and potential road users, secondly possible reductions in accidents and thirdly any cost savings to drivers because of lower maintenance costs. It will be recognised that these benefits differ in two respects from the costs. Firstly, they are, with the exception of reduced maintenance costs, non-monetary benefits and secondly they occur over the whole life of the road not just in one particular year.

In order to compare non-monetary benefits occurring over many years with monetary costs occurring at the start of a project the former have to be converted into monetary terms and discounted. In the case of a new road the values used for time lost varies according to whether it is working time or leisure time but can perhaps be up to £1 per man hour. Hence if a new road were built saving 500 travellers one hour each then the time savings benefit might be up to £500. Again if it is thought that there were likely to be a reduction in the number of accidents then it is also possible to value loss of life or serious injury and these could also be included into the calculation. Finally, any reduced maintenance costs could be included.

These continuous benefits have to be compared with the initial capital costs in the building of the road (and any subsequent extra maintenance costs). For such a comparison the method of discounting is used. This assumes that £1 today is more valuable than the certain promise of £1 in a year's time by the amount of the interest that the £1 could accumulate during the year. Thus, if the rate of interest is assumed to be 10% then £1 today is worth £1.10 in one year and £1.21 in two years.

The discounted benefits of a project must then exceed the costs of the project.

Hence if C = present costs
bi = benefit in year (i)
N = life of project
r = rate of interest

then

$$C > \sum_{i=1}^{N} \frac{bi}{(1+r)^N}$$

The weaknesses of the approach are many, the attaching of monetary values to non-monetary benefits being the most contentious, but it is at least a first attempt to improve decision-making in the public sector and does identify a method of approaching problems which is certainly an improvement on the ad hoc approach employed in the past.

6. Explain elasticity of demand, and discuss the factors which can affect the elasticity of demand for a good or service. (S)

Elasticity of demand is the responsiveness of demand for a product to changes in price. A numerical value can be derived if elasticity is defined as the percentage change in quantity demanded for a one per cent change in price. The following formula can be used if there is a very small change, proportionate to the original price, in the price:

$$\text{Elasticity of demand} = \frac{\text{Proportionate change in the demand}}{\text{Proportionate change in the Price}}$$

If the result is greater than unity, then demand is said to be elastic at that price; if it is less than unity demand is said to be inelastic at that price; if the result is unity then demand is said to be of unit elasticity.

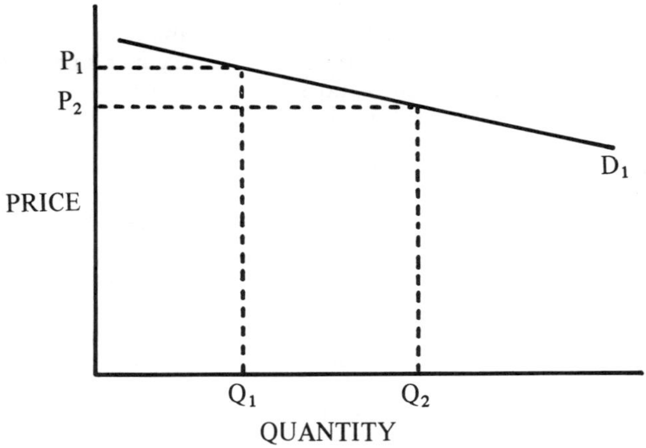

In the diagram above D_1 is the demand curve and the diagram illustrates an elastic demand for a product since a reduction in price from P_1 to P_2 results in a more than proportionate increase in quality demanded from Q_{21} to Q_2. Elastic demand curves are normally fairly flat.

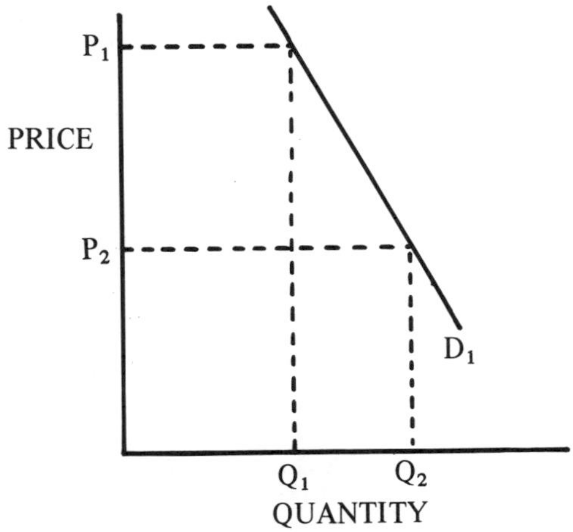

In the diagram above D_1 again represents the demand curve. Here a considerable reduction in price results in only a small increase in the quantity demanded. An inelastic demand curve normally slopes quite sharply down to the right.

The two limiting cases of these curves are the horizontal and vertical demand curves. The horizontal demand curve is perfectly elastic and assumes that price does not have to be reduced to increase output. Elasticity in this case is infinite. Where the demand curve slopes down vertically then no matter how much price is reduced the quantity sold remains constant. Here elasticity is zero.

Several factors can affect the elasticity of demand for a good or service. If competition is fierce and substitutes close, then a small reduction in price is likely to result in a more than proportionate increase in sales. The stronger the competition the more elastic the demand curve. This is illustrated in discussions on perfect competition where the demand curve is assumed to be horizontal.

The proportion of income spent on a good influences elasticity of demand. If the proportion is small – such as on salt – then a 50% increase in price is likely to result in only a small reduction in the amount demanded because it affects only marginally the purchaser's overall income. Conversely if the proportion of income spent on a product is large, demand is likely to be very elastic.

It is also important to differentiate between "luxuries" and "necessities". The demand for the former is far more elastic than that for the latter and therefore increases in the price of luxuries will result in substantial reductions in demand. However, this is open to considerable dispute. Empirical studies have found substantially varying price elasticities irrespective of whether they could be classified as luxuries or necessities. In fact elasticity is probably more highly correlated with the generality with which a good is bought i.e. the demand for daily papers of the popular type is far more elastic than the demand for "The Times".

The demand for habit forming goods is often highly inelastic. Classically, government duties which add small amounts to the prices of cigarettes and beer make very little difference to the amounts demanded.

7. Explain carefully what you understand by:
(a) The price-elasticity of demand for a good.
(b) The income-elasticity of demand for a good.
(c) The cross-elasticity of demand for a good. (L)

(a) Price elasticity of demand is a measure of the responsiveness of demand to changes in price. When, as the result of a relatively small change in price, there is a relatively large change in demand, demand is said to be elastic. Conversely, demand is said to be inelastic when little or no change results from a change in price, however large that change. Price elasticity of demand is capable of simple mathematical measurement.

Price Elasticity of Demand

$$= \frac{\text{Proportionate change in Demand}}{\text{Proportionate change in Price}}$$

Figures greater than unity show that demand is price elastic whereas figures less than unity show that demand is price inelastic.

(b) It is also possible to measure the change in the demand for a commodity following a change in income. This is known as the income elasticity of demand. Again it can be measured:–

Income Elasticity of Demand

$$= \frac{\text{Proportionate change in Demand}}{\text{Proportionate change in Income}}$$

An increase in income can be followed by an increase or a decrease in the demand for a commodity. Likewise a fall in income can be followed by an increase or a decrease in the demand for a commodity. Hence in considering income elasticity of demand, the nature of the changes must always be made clear.

Income elasticity is a useful concept. If the income elasticities for twin tub washing machines and automatic washing machines is known, it would be possible to predict the fall in the quantity demanded of the former and the rise in the quantity demand of the latter following a given rise in workers' incomes.

(c) It is also possible to measure the change in demand for a commodity following changes in the price of another commodity. This is known as cross elasticity of demand. It is capable of measurement by the formula:

Cross Elasticity of Demand

$$= \frac{\text{Proportionate change in Demand for X}}{\text{Proportionate change in Price of Y}}$$

If X and Y are regarded as close substitutes, the amount of X demanded will increase as a result of an increase in the price of Y. In this case the figure for elasticity will be positive. Butter and margarine are classic examples of this. If X and Y are in joint demand – as with cars and petrol – the amount of X (say, cars) demanded will decrease as a result of an increase in price of Y (say, petrol). In such a case the figure for elasticity is negative.

8. You have the sole concession to sell sandwiches at a Pop Festival. Each costs 5p (including all relevant costs such as that of your labour). From previous experience your best estimate of the demand is the following

Price (p)						
9	9½	10	10½	11	11½	12
Sales (per day)						
2400	2200	2000	1800	1600	1400	1200

You aim to maximise your profits. Assuming your estimate to be accurate,

(a) Calculate the elasticity of demand on this demand schedule around the price of 10p. Explain precisely the concept of elasticity you use.

(b) How many sandwiches would you sell in a day and at what price?

(c) Suppose that one hour before you leave you find that you have 400 sandwiches left which will be inedible at the end of the afternoon. Your estimates have proved wrong. You now estimate that the following demand schedule faces you

Price (p)	7	6	5	4	3	2
Sales (per hour)	100	150	200	300	350	400

What price would you now charge and how many (if any) sandwiches would be left unsold? (L)

(a) Elasticity of demand around a price of 10p

Elasticity of demand

$$= \frac{\text{Proportionate change in quantity demand}}{\text{Proportionate change in price}}$$

When price increases from 10p to 10½p, proportionate increase is 5%. At 10½p proportionate decrease in quantity demanded falls from 2000 to 1800, a decrease of 10%.

$$\therefore \text{Elasticity of demand} = \frac{10\%}{5\%} = 2$$

Conversely if price decreased from 10p to 9½p, this is a decrease of 5%. At 9½p quantity demanded increases from 2000 to 2200, an increase of 10%.

$$\therefore \text{Elasticity of demand} = \frac{10\%}{5\%} = 2$$

(b) If the object is to maximise profits, then this stage is reached when the difference between total revenue and total costs is at its greatest.

Price	Sales	Total Rev.	Total Costs	Profit
9	2400	21600	12000	9600
9½	2200	20900	11000	9900
10	2000	20000	10000	10000
10½	1800	18900	9000	9900
11	1600	17600	8000	9600
11½	1400	16100	7000	9100
12	1200	14400	6000	8400

Profit is maximised at £100 (10000p) and the price necessary to produce that profit is 10p and the number of sandwiches sold at that price is 2000.

(c) 400 sandwiches are left. These have already been produced at a cost of 400 x 5p = 2000p. A loss is inevitable and a price must be fixed to give the greatest total revenue (and hence the smallest total loss). Given the demand schedule, the total revenue at a price of 7p is 700p, at 6p is 900p, at 5p is 1000p, at 4p is 1200p, at 3p is 1050p, at 2p is 800p. Hence, price to be charged is 4p leaving 100 unsold.

9. What is meant by the *elasticity of supply?* Upon what circumstances will the elasticity of supply of any good chiefly depend? (O)

Supply, in economics, is the amount of a good offered for sale at one time and one particular price. The Law of Supply states that rising prices tend to expand supply, while falling prices tend to reduce it. The Law of Supply expresses only a broad tendency, for the readiness of supplies of commodities to respond to changes in price depends on the nature of the good itself. The supply of some commodities – for example car shampoos – can be readily adjusted to price changes, whilst in other cases – for example meat – supply can only be adjusted over a long period, if at all. Supply that increases or decreases readily in response to price changes is said to be elastic; when it does not respond readily to price changes supply is said to be inelastic. The elasticity of supply can be numerically measured by the formula:

$$\text{Elasticity of supply} = \frac{\text{Proportionate change in quantity supplied}}{\text{Proportionate change in Price}}$$

If both proportions are the same, then elasticity is unity. If elasticity is greater than unity, supply is elastic; if it is less than unity it is inelastic.

It has already been noted that the elasticity of supply depends on the nature of the good itself. The supply of goods that cannot be stored is inelastic because if the price rises no more can be brought forward for sale at any particular time, and, if the price falls, the supply cannot be reduced without involving a total loss on the amount unsold.

The production of some commodities – such as cattle, grain, buses – takes a long time and their supply can only be varied after the time taken to produce them has elapsed. Supply in such cases is inelastic.

Where production involves large capital outlay i.e. heavy *fixed* costs of production, supply, beyond the full capacity of the existing concerns with their existing equipment, is inelastic.

Concerns will not incur the large expense involved in expansion and new ones will not be set up until it is fairly certain that the higher price is likely to continue. Up to the full productive capacity of existing plant and premises, and as more *variable* factors are engaged, supply may be elastic for goods that can be produced in a short time. Cotton mills, for example, can be fully or partly used for the production of cotton cloth, according to the market conditions prevailing, but no extension of the mills would be undertaken as a result of an increase in price until a long period of full working had been experienced.

If producers can produce for stock as well as for supply, supply tends to be elastic, for the goods will be stored rather than brought forward for sale when price is low. If goods can be transferred easily from one market to another, supply tends to be elastic. The supply of manufactured goods that are durable and involve only relatively simple processes of production and processes that are of relatively short duration – for example mops – exhibits the most marked degree of elasticity. The supply of natural products – for example timber – is markedly inelastic, while supply that is fixed – for example antiques – is inelastic.

It will have been noted that running through the factors affecting elasticity of supply is the concept of *time*. In the short-run fixed factors of production – for example machinery and plant – remain constant and supply can only be altered by altering the variable factors of production such as labour and raw materials. In the long run, all factors of production – both fixed and variable – can be altered and hence so can supply. The length of the short period and of the long period differs from product to product as has been seen.

10. Explain the distinction between a movement along a supply curve and a shift of such a curve. (L)

The price of any commodity can alter without any change in the underlying conditions of supply. This in fact occurs when there has been a change in the underlying conditions of demand and the demand curve has shifted. The supply curve remains in the same position and the change in price has caused an extension of supply if the price has risen or a contraction of supply if the price has fallen. Such extensions and contractions of supply are called movements *along* a supply curve. A movement along a supply curve to the right indicates an extension of supply and an increase in the quantity supplied. On the other hand, a movement along a supply curve to the left indicates a contraction of supply and a decrease in the quantity supplied.

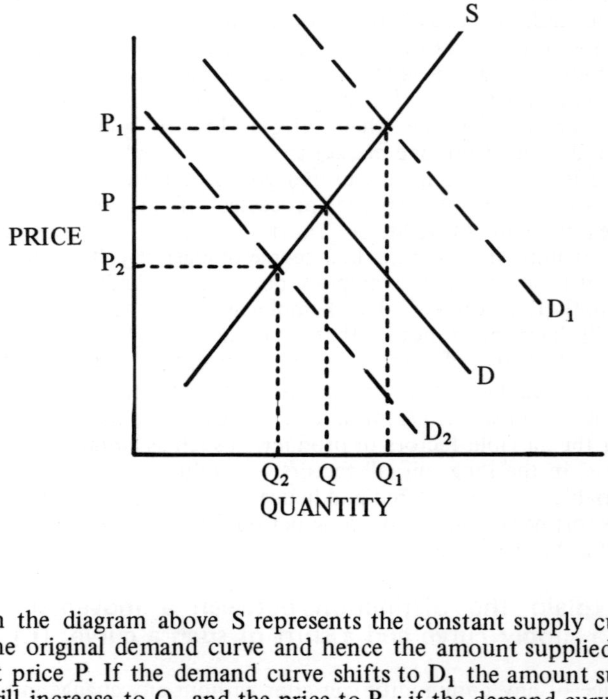

In the diagram above S represents the constant supply curve, D the original demand curve and hence the amount supplied was Q at price P. If the demand curve shifts to D_1 the amount supplied will increase to Q_1 and the price to P_1; if the demand curve shifts to D_2 the amount supplied will decrease to Q_2 and the price to P_2.

However, the price of a commodity can alter because of a change in the underlying conditions of supply – for example, a change in the costs of production. When because of this more is supplied at each and every price supply is said to have increased. The supply curve is now shifted to the right. When less is supplied at each and every price supply is said to have decreased. The supply curve is now shifted to the left.

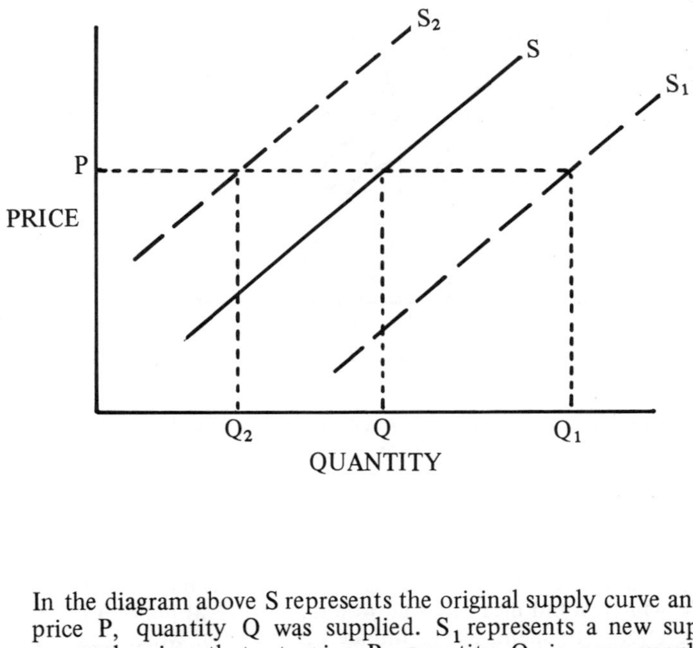

In the diagram above S represents the original supply curve and at price P, quantity Q was supplied. S_1 represents a new supply curve showing that at price P, quantity Q_1 is now supplied. Likewise S_2 represents another supply curve showing that at price P again, quantity Q_2 is now supplied. The curve shifts from S to S_1 as the conditions of supply have allowed supply at price P to be increased to Q_1; the curve shifts from S to S_2 as the conditions of supply have allowed supply at price P to be decreased to Q_2.

11. Distinguish between the income and substitution effects of a change in the price of butter.

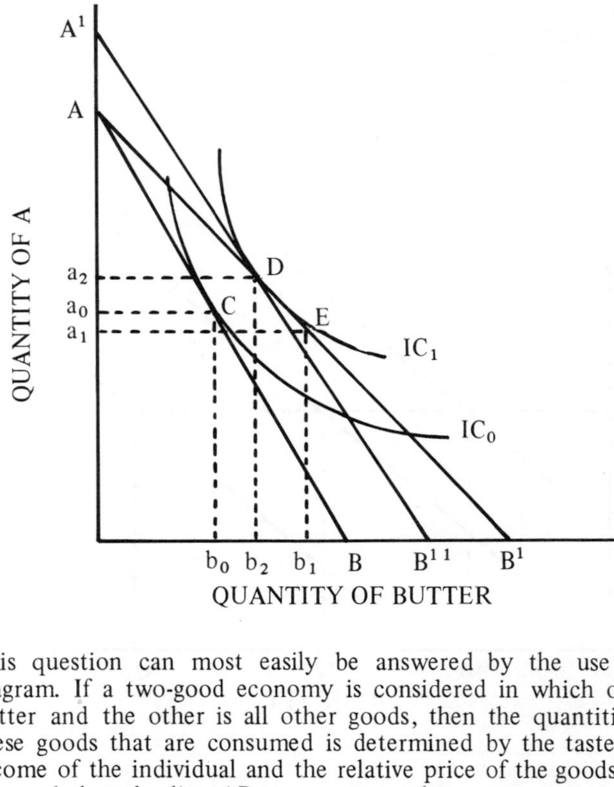

This question can most easily be answered by the use of a diagram. If a two-good economy is considered in which one is butter and the other is all other goods, then the quantities of these goods that are consumed is determined by the tastes and income of the individual and the relative price of the goods. It is assumed that the line AB represents total income constraint i.e. the individual could choose to spend all his income on "other" goods which would mean that he would consume at point A or he could choose to spend all his money on butter in which case he would consume quantity B. In fact it is more likely that the individual will consume some combination of both butter and all other goods, but he will, in the absence of an increase in income, be unable to consume combinations to the right of the AB line. The exact combination chosen is determined by his own tastes which are represented by the indifference curve IC_0 which is tangential to the AB line and which illustrates that b_0 quantity of butter is demanded and a_0 quantity of other goods. An indifference curve notes the preferences or tastes of an individual and is defined so that the individual is indifferent to all combinations of both goods along the line. Utility is thus unaffected by movements along an indifference curve and is only increased by movements on to new curves (increases in utility are normally shown by a movement of the curve to the right and decreases by movements to the left). The individual will therefore try to move to the indifference curve furthest to the right in the diagram but he is still constrained by income. In fact this is illustrated by assuming that IC_0 is tangential to AB at C and it is assumed that he maximises his utility with combinations a_0 of other goods and b_0 of butter.

If it is now postulated that the price of butter falls then more butter can be purchased from the same level of income. There are two distinguishable constituents of such a price reduction which are identified as the income and substitution effects. Thus in the case of a fall in the price of butter there will be more butter consumed because it has become more attractive relative to other goods. We may therefore imagine butter having been substituted for other goods. However it is unlikely that all the saving in expenditure on butter will be taken up by an increased quantity demanded – for this to be the case an elasticity of demand for butter of unity would have to be assumed. If elasticity were less than unity this would mean that some money would be left over to spend on other goods. Therefore a reduction in the price of any one good will result in effectively an increase in real income to consumer. In the case of butter the increase in real income is likely to be small because even a substantial fall in the price of butter, is only a relatively small component of total expenditure and will have only a marginal effect on real income. Precisely the same analysis can be applied to a rise in the price of butter. Here a rise in the price of butter results effectively in a fall in real income which will also have an effect on other goods, expenditure on which may also fall.

The effect of a fall in the price of butter is illustrated in the diagram. Here the quantity of butter that can be bought with its fall in price increases from B to B_1. It is assumed that tastes remain unaffected by such a price change and that the new indifference curve IC_1 which is tangential to the new income constraint AB_1 is of similar shape to IC_0, and is tangential at the point E. Thus it can be seen that as expected the quantity of butter demanded has increased, as a result of the fall in price from b_o to b_3 and the quantity of other goods demanded has risen, by the lesser amount from a_o to a_1. In order to determine how much of the increase in quantity demanded is attributable to income and how much to substitution effect the new line A^1B^{11} is drawn which is parallel to the old AB line, and represents the real increase in income caused by the butter price fall. It is therefore parallel to the old AB line because it assumes that the relative prices of all goods remains the same. Again assuming that tastes remain unchanged the consumer will, with increased income but relative prices unchanged, demand a different quantity of butter and in fact the new income constraint line A^1B^{11} is tangential to the indifference curve IC_1 at D where quantity b_2 of butter is demanded, b_2-b_o is attributable to the increased income and is the income effect and b_1-b_2 is the substitution effect, with b_1-b_o being the total increase in butter demanded as a result of the price fall. As noted earlier exactly the same analysis can be applied to an increase in price.

In conclusion we note that a fall in the price of butter will result in an increase in the purchase of butter partly because income has increased and partly because the butter has become cheaper relative to other goods. The first former is referred to as the income effect and the latter as the substitution effect.

12.

Price of X per ton (£s):	**1**	**2**	**3**	**4**	**5**
Demand for X per period (tons):	**25**	**16**	**12**	**10**	**9**
Supply of X per period (tons):	**3**	**12**	**12**	**14**	**29**

Given the above data concerning the demand for and supply of X in a given market:

(a) What would be the free market price of X?

(b) What would be the price if demand increased by 4 tons at every price?

(c) What would be the effect of a government's imposing a minimum price of £5 per ton in the original situation?

Explain your answers. (L)

(a) Free market price is where demand equals supply i.e. £3.

(b) Price if demand increased by 4 tons at every price would be where new demand equals supply i.e. £4 since the demand and supply will now both be 14 tons.

(c) If the government imposed a minimum price of £5 per ton this price would be above the free market equilibrium. If prices are held at this level suppliers are willing to produce more of the commodity than can be absorbed by the market. It will thus create a surplus of unsold stocks. This situation can be dealt with by subsidising exports of X so that the goods are sold at very low prices overseas. Alternatively the surplus of X can be destroyed or be given away in foreign aid programmes. A further possibility is for the government to establish production quotas for individual suppliers so that they each produce less than they would wish to produce at the government fixed minimum price.

13. Discuss the merits and demerits of a price system as a means of allocating resources. (L)

The economy of a country produces differing quantities of different goods. In the Western world the pricing mechanism, in part, determines what, and how many, goods will be produced and how these goods will be allocated to consumers once they have been produced. The objective of the pricing system is to carry out these functions cheaply and equitably.

The pricing system operates on the assumption that there is a relative scarcity of most goods i.e. there are more people wanting the goods than there are goods available. For virtually every good there is an excess of demand over supply.

People's demand for goods is determined in part by their income and in part by their taste. They must allocate their limited expenditure to those goods which yield them the highest utility or satisfaction. The demand for one good is, therefore, the combination of the whole community's constrained preferences.

In the diagram the demand curve (D_1) shows that as price falls so the amount of the good that will be demanded will rise. Price (P_1) resulting in a quantity (Q_1) being sold, is derived at the point when the demand curve (D_1) and the supply curve (S_1) cross. The supply curve shows that as the price rises suppliers are prepared to supply more at the higher price. It is logical that P_1 represents a satisfactory price where buyers are prepared to buy the amount that the sellers are prepared to sell.

The price at which the good is sold is unlikely in a free market system to be below the cost that the producer has incurred in producing it plus some element of profit to compensate for doing

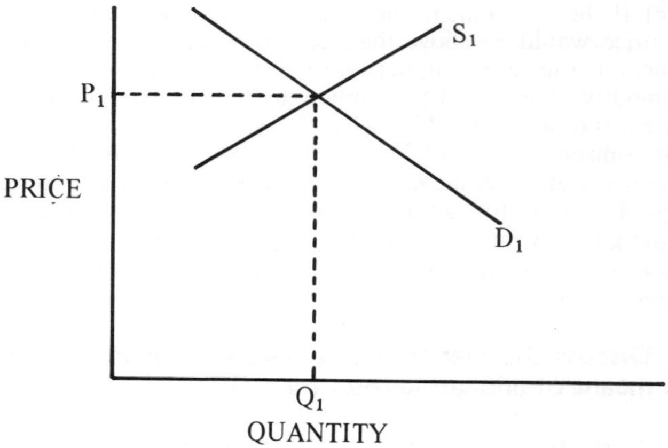

the job. Because few are philanthropists, the pricing system determines which goods are produced.

The pricing system also determines the distribution of goods, through the distribution of wealth either in the form of wages or profit. To take the example of wages, the levels of which are again the product of supply and demand interaction in the labour market: if on the diagram P_1 represents the wage rate (the price of labour) then Q_1 units of labour will be supplied.

The merits of a price system are that, if it works properly, it is an objective means of allocating resources. It does not require decisions to be made by politicians on which goods it is "desirable" to produce nor what is a "desirable" distribution of income. Instead it is assumed that desirability is demonstrated by demand and that if people want a good they will be prepared to pay for it.

There are disadvantages of a price system and because of these it is very unusual for a pure price system to be practised. The price system takes no account of profit or corporate goods, for which there is obviously a need but one that cannot be demonstrated through the pricing system. An example of this is national defence which it would be impossible for an individual to purchase, though he may wish for his country to be protected from foreign aggressors. The governments of most countries decide on the amount of money that will be spent on defence, on roads, on the health service, on education, in conjunction with other public expenditure for which taxes are collected.

Another disadvantage of the price system is that it encourages the pursuit of profit and self-interest and results, in some people's minds, in an inequitable distribution of wealth. The alternative is to have some government agency determining a more "equitable" distribution of income and production of more "desirable" goods.

In times of considerable scarcity of essential goods e.g. sugar in wartime, the price system left unadulterated would mean that very many people went without the essentials. In such times systems of rationing, price controls and government intervention have to be introduced to prevent the price system working against the obvious advantage of the majority of the population.

A further defect of the price system is that the price at which a good is sold does not take account of the full costs of producing that good, but merely those incurred by the entrepreneur. For example, a plant owned by A may produce bricks for which the owner will fix a price to take account of the costs of production plus an element of profit. As a by-product, A's plant may generate fluoride resulting in reduced milk yield in cattle owned by a neighbouring farmer, B. If B is unable to obtain compensation from A then this means that the real cost of bricks is understated by the pricing mechanism, and the real cost of milk may be overstated. This effect is known as an externality and can result in serious distortions to the market pricing system, especially where no means of direct compensation is available.

In Western democracies it is customary to accept the pricing mechanism as the basic allocator of scarce resources but to intervene where it is thought that the mechanism does not work effectively.

14. Explain what is meant by "consumer surplus". What are the economic applications of this concept?

The concept of consumer surplus was introduced by Alfred Marshall in the late nineteenth century. It was based on the assumption of diminishing marginal utility, and has proved to be the basis for much of the welfare economics that is applied today.

It is assumed that the demand curve for a product slopes downwards. This means that as the price of a product falls, then the quantity demanded will rise. In practice, most demand curves follow this pattern. In general, however, the price of a good is determined equally by the costs of producing the good and price is fixed where the demand and supply curves cross. In the diagram below D represents the demand curve and this crosses the demand curve such that a price P is produced and a quantity Q is demanded at this price.

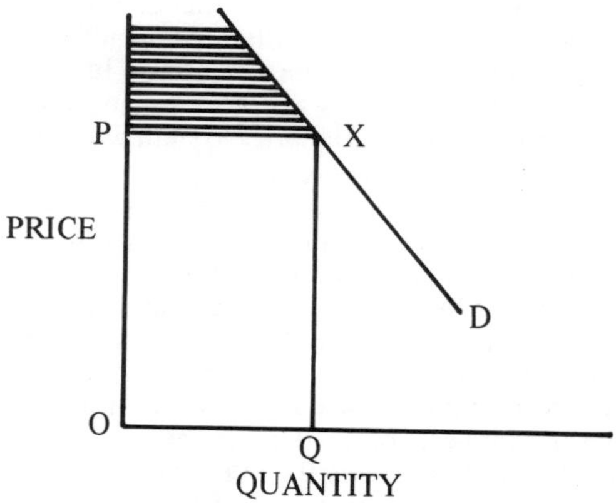

At this price there are a number of consumers who would have been prepared to pay more than the market price and will buy the good until, to them, price equals their marginal utility. The area above PX in the diagram is the utility which is not paid for by the consumer known as consumer surplus. This can be seen by imagining that the total utility derived by consumers when Q goods are purchased is the area under the demand curve. Of this, however, consumers only pay PXQ and therefore the remaining area above the line PX can be regarded as the consumer surplus.

A number of criticisms may be made of this concept, most deriving from criticisms of the theory of diminishing marginal utility. For example any theory of diminishing marginal utility must run contrary to the everyday observation that expectations probably rise faster than the ability to satisfy them. Thus with increasing income there is probably a more than proportionate increase in the desire to purchase consumer durables. However a demand curve for one particular consumer durable may well slope downwards provided that income and tastes remain unchanged. Provided therefore that the demand curve does slope down to the right then there will always be consumer surplus.

The applications of consumer surplus analysis have been dogged, however, by the difficulty of overcoming arguments about the marginal utility of money. This is because formulating a demand curve in terms of money may not reveal people's true preferences but merely those which are constrained by income.

In recent years in the field of social economics the concept of consumer surplus has been used. It has been increasingly recognised that the market value was not indicative of the "true" value of certain commodities. Probably the most famous application of this was in the Roskill Commission report on the Third London Airport. Here, an attempt was made to examine the effect of noise on people's homes, and it became increasingly realised that frequently the value of a house to the occupant was considerably in excess of the market price. Thus it was important if an estimate was to be made of the real cost of noise (possibly resulting in the occupant having to sell his house) that the element of consumer surplus was estimated as this might be lost in a move to alternative property.

Again there are difficulties over the marginal utility of money. Thus, if the question is asked as to how much the house owner is prepared to pay to avoid noise, this sum is obviously affected by his income, and his other expenses. Willingness to pay is not therefore an accurate estimation of the area of the consumer surplus, and in fact to estimate this area the Commission asked occupiers to put monetary values on their homes which would exactly compensate them for having to move out.

15. How is the general level of retail prices measured? What difficulties arise in making measurements of this kind? (L)

The general level of retail prices is measured by the Retail Prices Index (RPI) which is published monthly by the Department of Employment. It is calculated in respect of prices on one selected Tuesday in each month, normally between the 16th and 22nd of that month.

Because the RPI measures price changes only, it is essential to collect prices for the same goods and services each month. It can be pictured as calculating the cost of a large and representative 'basket' of goods and services in January each year and finding the cost of the same 'basket' in each of the 12 following months. The percentage increase in the cost since January can then be calculated. The 'basket' is changed each January so that it is as up-to-date as possible. In practice the total cash cost of the 'basket' of goods and services is not calculated each month. It is simpler to calculate for each item the percentage change in price per pound, per pint etc. and to combine these separate percentage changes into a single 'all-items' average percentage change by the use of 'weights'. Some items are more important than others. For example, most households spend more on bread than on soap. So a 10% increase in the price of bread will clearly add more to the cost of the fixed 'basket' than a similar increase in the price of soap. Each percentage change in price is given a 'weight' to represent its relative importance in household spending in the previous January and the percentage change in prices is multiplied by these weights before being averaged. The method gives the same answer as if the total money cost of the fixed 'basket' of goods and services were compared with the total cost of the same 'basket' in the previous January. The weights, which are revised each January, are derived from the latest year's results of the continuous Family Expenditure Survey (FES).

A long list of items goes into the average 'basket' which is bought by United Kingdom households. The items are divided into 11 broad groups. These groups (together with their weights for January 1975) are:–

Food 23.2
Transport and Vehicles 14.9
Housing 10.8
Clothing and Footwear 8.9
Alcoholic drink 8.2
Miscellaneous goods 7.1
Fuel and light 5.3
Durable household goods 7.0
Services 5.2
Meals out 4.8
Tobacco 4.6

These weights total 100. All groups are split into a number of sections (e.g. food is broken down into 32 sections). Prices are regularly obtained for nearly 350 separate commodities and services in each of 200 areas. In each area the price of a particular item is collected in up to five shops so that for each item up to 1,000 prices are collected all over the country.

Such measurements are, however, difficult to make and to make accurately. Moreover, once such measurements have been made they are often incorrectly interpreted and can, of course, be mis-used and this itself is a difficulty which arises when such measurements are made. Many people see the RPI as a Cost of Living Index which it is not. Many other factors – apart from the general level of retail prices – enter into the cost of living e.g. taxes, national insurance payments and benefits, social services etc.

One of the main difficulties centres around the definition of the average family and hence the average 'basket' of goods. The average family is a myth and hence, to some extent, is the average 'basket' of goods and services and the more people differ from the average, the more meaningless does the RPI become. It also measures the general level of retail prices whereas often *particular* prices are more important to individuals: average prices may rise while goods of peculiar significance to a certain individual may fall.

Furthermore, whilst it might be relatively easy to measure changes in the prices of commodities it is too difficult to link this up with changes in quality. Lettuces may fall in price this week from 20p to 15p but if the quality has fallen to the extent that it is now necessary to buy two lettuces instead of one the total expenditure has increased by 50% whereas prices have fallen by 25%. The latter will be reflected in RPI whereas the former – which is more important – will not be so reflected.

All commodities are not of equal importance and this produces a difficulty which 'weighting' has attempted to overcome. Prices vary considerably from shop to shop, town to town, area to area but this problem has been met to some extent by taking up to 1000 prices per article. These are major difficulties and attempts have been made to minimise their effect but this can never be fully achieved. The weights themselves are fixed in January from information from previous year's FES and hence these weights by December could be something like two years out of date and in an age of as much change as ours, two years is a very long time.

16. What are the advantages and disadvantages of vertical integration? (L)

Vertical integration is the amalgamation of several companies engaged in the consecutive stages of an industry from the production of the raw material to the finished product. If a tyre company, for example, establishes a subsidiary company to acquire a rubber plantation in Malaysia, another company to grow cotton in East Africa, and a third to spin and weave its own cotton into cloth, and so on, in order to control the production of the component parts required to make a complete motor-car tyre, the combination is said to be "vertical". The greatest advantage lies in the elimination of intermediate profits, but the tendency is for the combination to become unwieldy and unmanageable.

The main objective and the outstanding advantage of vertical integration is the obtaining of greater control over the whole production process. For example a large engineering company might purchase parts from a smaller company, but have reason to be dissatisfied with the quality. The alternatives that face it are either to manufacture the parts themselves or to gain control over the supplier. Obviously the same logic could apply to a firm which was dissatisfied with the way its product was being marketed. In any event, vertical integration would give the advantage of a greater control over the production process. This, of course, leads to another advantage of vertical integration in that it can result in a firm guaranteeing the supply of some essential product for itself and ensuring that its competitors are not so supplied. The firm integrates backwards in order to secure direct control over the supply of its raw materials and hence has the advantage of reducing one of the major risks a firm faces – that of failure of supplies. This leads to two other advantages for the firm. First, it is protected against the damaging effect of a rise in the price of raw materials; secondly, it avoids the danger that they may come under the control of a competitor.

Vertical integration also enables firms to benefit from the technical economy of scale arising from linked processes. In steel-making, for example, linked processes make for the conservation of heat and a saving, therfore, in fuel and power. Many factories make their own boxes or tins for the finished product, and consequently save time and transport costs.

A vertically integrated firm enjoys various other advantages. It can effect economies of unified control of the succeeding stages of production. If each stage is in separate ownership, the chain of independent firms may hang back from innovations which are in the common interest of the group, but from which the innovator derives little advantage. Integration enables the conflicting interests of the various stages of production to be reconciled: each firm's special knowledge can be pooled and new processes of common advantage can be introduced. Integration, therefore, introduces more comprehensive planning.

Vertical integration is often a method of extending monopoly from one stage of production to another which of course yields an advantage to the vertically integrated firm.

The trend towards vertical integration is much less powerful than the trend towards horizontal integration. It is obstructed by lack of familiarity with the technique of other stages of production and by lack of capital with which to finance vertical integration. Above all, it is obstructed by the forces which make for the specialisation of firms on a narrow range of processes. Disintegration goes on side by side with integration as one industrial process after another reaches the scale at which it can be turned over to specialist firms. This, together with the unwieldy and often unmanageable size of the combination, produces disadvantages for the vertically integrated firm.

17. "The nature of the product is the main determinant of the size of firms in an industry." Discuss.

At any one time in most industries there are a combination of both small and large firms. But certain industries are dominated by a few large firms whereas others have many small firms serving only local markets. Thus, the oil and petrol industry is dominated by a few giants whereas the building industry is a mass of firms many of which employ under ten permanent staff.

This variety in the size of firm is largely determined by the size and characteristics of the market being served, and the extent of any economies of scale that may exist. These economies are defined to exist when the marginal long run cost of production falls with increasing output. Such economies will become available, either or both, to the firm and to its competitors, and serve to increase the size of the firm. The greater the economies of scale the larger the likely size of firm. Examples of external economies of scale (i.e. accruing to all firms) are the introduction of specialist banking services to an area specialising in one type of production, i.e. the textile areas of Lancashire in nineteenth century England had their own banks from which they could generally obtain credit. Other economies include the provision of a specialist labour force trained in the ways of the industry. More important, are the internal economies of scale. These are primarily determined by the nature of the market being served.

It is assumed in economic theory that it is the objective of the entrepreneur to maximise profits. Thus, it is obvious that if the marginal cost curve slopes downwards, i.e. marginal cost falls with output then, provided demand is unchanged, more will be

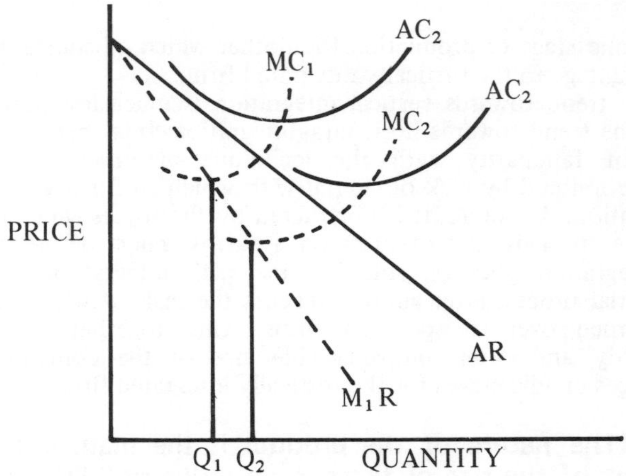

demanded at a lower price. In the diagram when marginal cost equals marginal revenue, $MC_1 = MR$, output is at level Q_1. With an increase in output to Q_2 marginal cost may well fall and a new point of equilibrium determined. In this case the increase in production results in a "step" economy, though the point could equally well be illustrated by a movement along a downward sloping marginal cost curve.

In practice there are a number of factors that can produce economies of scale. For example Adam Smith in his pin factory found that by specialisation of labour, with each employee concentrating on one particular aspect of production, productivity could be greatly improved over the previous system of each employee carrying out all the processes of pin making. However the nature of the final product determines the extent of such economies. Thus, though such mechanisation is possible on factory conveyor belts it is less suited to the tertiary or service industry where the nature of the service provided is on sale rather than a physical good. Even in the service industries there does appear to be an increasing tendency for the average size of firms to be increasing. Recent years have seen a revolution in the distributive trades with the growth of the supermarket and even the hypermarket at the expense of the local store. Large distributors have found manufacturers willing to sell them large quantities of stock at below normal price because of the reliability of their demand. This has encouraged small firms to combine together for purchasing while maintaining their retailing independence. Production economies of scale are one main reason for large firms dominating some manufacturing industries.

Some products such as pharmaceuticals, are the product of many years intense research and development on the part of chemical companies. Today, few new companies could consider competing with the international giants in this sector. Virtually all such companies have patents on the products once marketed and are able to charge high prices which enable them to recoup safely the money outlaid on research. Again the nature of the product determines that only large firms are able to produce it.

It would be an oversimplification to regard the final product as the only factor determining the size of firms in an industry. There are internal economies of size in many industries irrespective of the final product. Such economies are usually divided between technical, which have been discussed above, and managerial and financial. Managerial economies arise from the fact that it is not necessary to increase management expenses with each increase in production. Financial economies occur to the larger firm because it is probably more financially secure to a banker and more credit-worthy than its smaller competitor. In fact, the small-medium firm today still has considerable difficulty raising capital (the so-called MacMillan Gap).

It would be equally naive to assume that it was always advantageous to be large. As noted earlier the service industries are still primarily dominated by the small firm where none of the above economies is sufficient to outweigh the disadvantages of loss of identity in the monolithic organisation. The small firm will continue to thrive in those areas again where the market is too small to yield significant economies and or where the personal touch in service is required.

Two other points should be made. Firstly it has been assumed so far that the entrepreneur's objective is to maximise profit. This may not in fact be the case. He may be seeking to achieve other objectives such as the maintenance of a satisfactory profit level combined with "a quiet life". Other objectives include the maintenance of family control which is far more important in Britain than in the U.S.A. (Of the largest forty British firms, twenty-six were family controlled whereas there were only six of the top forty U.S. companies still under family control).

Finally the state often plays a part in determining the size of companies in the U.K. During the 1960's the Labour government operated two bodies with apparently contradictory aims – the Industrial Reorganisation Corporation to encourage mergers in industries where efficiency was low due to the small scale of operations, and the Monopolies Commission set up in 1956 to examine those industries which were dominated by a single industry to what might have been to the detriment of the consumer. Though, of course, in apparent contradiction the two bodies were applying themselves to different industries existing side by side in the economy.

It is only in part true to say that the nature of product determines the structure of the industry. The state and technology also play their part. In a dynamic economy new firms, who will inevitably be small, are always being spawned. Equally, technology may transform an industry so that although previously it consisted of many small firms, it becomes increasingly dominated by its larger competitors.

18. What factors determine the rewards distributed to factors of production?

There are four factors of production; Land, Labour, Capital and Entreprenneurial skill. The rewards to these factors take the form of rent on land and wages, interest and quasi-rent in the other three respectively.

The rewards paid can be understood in simple demand and supply terms and in fact the same type of analysis can be applied to all factors. For the sake of exposition the case of labour will be examined.

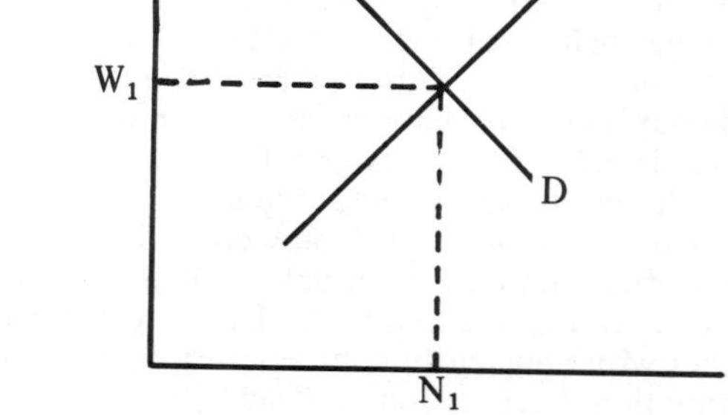

The interaction of supply of and demand for labour results in the setting of a price for labour. This is more commonly referred to as the wage rate and this is the level of reward to this factor. The wage (W_1) can be seen to depend therefore on the supply and demand. The demand for labour and all factors of production is a derived demand, i.e. it is determined by the demand for the product so that if the demand for the product should be reduced there will then be a compensating reduction in the demand for labour. Other factors which will influence the elasticity of demand for labour include the importance of labour, or any other factor, in the total cost of producing the product, and the ease of substituting one factor for another.

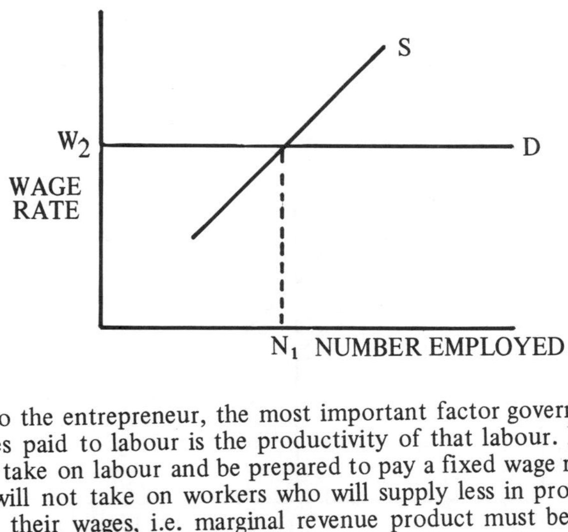

To the entrepreneur, the most important factor governing the wages paid to labour is the productivity of that labour. He may well take on labour and be prepared to pay a fixed wage rate W_2. He will not take on workers who will supply less in production than their wages, i.e. marginal revenue product must be greater than the market wage rate. The same principles can be applied to other factors such as land, i.e. the farmer will not pay more for new land than it is likely to be worth to him in terms of crop yields. The first premise of distribution theory is the marginal productivity theorem. On the other side is the concept of economic rent. This is an extra payment, because of its scarcity value, made to a factor. The concept as originally formulated by Ricardo was applied to land and rent was defined as the difference between payments for marginal land and that for non-marginal land. The difference was of course payment for the extra productivity of the land, but the concept (often described as quasi-rent in non-land instances) is now applied more generally. It is valid to regard any unique talent such as entrepreneurial ability as justification for payment above normal market rates, the difference between the two being regarded as ability rent.

In supply and demand terms, rent is the result of high demands for a service and an inelastic supply. Under situations of perfect competition and perfect substituteability such payments would not occur. However certain sites of land in the centres of large towns are unique and out of town sites are certainly not perfect substitutes and a difference in rents will therefore be levied. To illustrate, consider a pop group, the supply of which is perfectly inelastic, i.e. it is unique. We may regard D_1 as the demand for the groups services initially. Suppose the groups record suddenly becomes No. 1 in the "Charts" and demand shifts to D_2, but supply remains unchanged, i.e. they do not work more hours but simply charge a higher price. The rectangle W_1 W_2 AB is their economic rent.

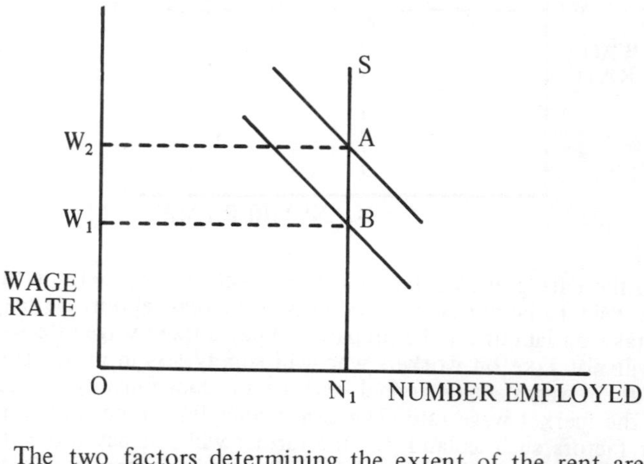

The two factors determining the extent of the rent are the demand for the services and the extent of any substituteability. There cannot be any rent in a situation of perfect competition i.e. in conditions where the demand curve is horizontal.

So far, discussion has been on a theoretical level. In practice the rewards paid are normally wages and salaries to labour and entrepreneur, rent for land and interest and profit on capital.

The theory of marginal productivity with regard to wages is often discounted by "practical men" who suggest that the employer has no idea of the productivity of the marginal worker and who suggest that wages paid are far more the result of trade union power in situations of collective bargaining. The power of trade unions can also be expressed in conventional economic terms, as it is effectively a monopolist restraining workers from accepting lower wage rates. It is unlikely that even a trade union could make all employers pay higher wages than marginal revenue product over a long period. The function of a trade union is to ensure that employers pay wages that approximate as nearly as possible to marginal revenue product.

Interest and profits are generally the payments to capital. The factors affecting these payments are firstly the demand for the final product and the nature of competition in the supply of the product. In the absence of competition the monopolist will earn above normal profits. Factors affecting interest rates include the propensity to save and the demand for investment opportunities which are in part determined by uncertainty, tastes and the business environment.

In conclusion, at the theoretical level, the rewards to factors of production are simply functions of the supply and demand for those factors. In practice such relationships are rather more complex.

19. What are the economic effects of immigration into the United Kingdom? (L – adapted)

As is frequently the case in Economics, it is useful to distinguish between short and long term effects. In the short term there can be substantial disturbances to the balance of payments for a number of reasons, depending whether immigrants come as single males or as family groups. If immigrants come as family groups – as has tended to be the case in the U.K. – and if the family is large it may need to be supported from public funds and may require the provision of social capital. Furthermore, the women and children of such a family will not work for some years. Any income is then used as the basis of demand for goods from the immigrants' native country which can impose strain on the exchange rate. If, however, the immigrant is a single male worker then in the short term he may send home substantial amounts of his salary in the form of remittances. This has the effect of reducing the level of aggregate demand in the immigrants' new country and possibly therefore reducing exchange rate pressures. To a country, therefore, with a balance of payments problem but no unemployment problem the single immigrant worker would appear to be more attractive than family immigration.

Secondly, in the short term, there is likely to be a redistribution of income towards capital and away from labour. This is because immigrant labour, which in many cases is relatively unskilled, is competing for jobs previously done by indigenous labour, resulting in generally lower wage rates. This means that indigenous capitalists benefit but that indigenous labour may be relatively worse off. If immigrant labour is relatively unskilled, indigenous labour may still benefit if the latter carry out the less well paid and less desirable jobs.

In the short term, because of the undesirable effect on the balance of payments, there is little doubt that immigration is economically undesirable for the recipient country. In the long term it is more difficult to be categorical on the net balance.

In part the effect depends on whether the immigrant is temporary or permanent. In many cases it is expensive to train foreign workers and it may also be expensive to attract them from their native lands by advertising. In the long term, if the immigrant stays he will tend to reduce his demand for goods imported from his homeland and will substitute goods produced in the country in which he works. It has also been found that the level of remittances is substantially reduced after the immigrant has been resident in a country for something like five years. This means that the balance of payments strain is substantially reduced. Over a number of years it is reasonable to postulate that an increase in immigration could result in substantial investment and act as an incentive for economic growth.

There may, of course, be other implications of immigration which, though not strictly economic, can have economic consequences. The density of the population of the U.K. is high and immigration increases this and the problems of congestion in the centre of urban areas are considerable – although it is argueable as to how far these would be significantly reduced by any restriction of immigration.

It is also suggested that the immigrant has economic consequences in the urban housing market because frequently an area of poor housing is taken over by immigrants resulting in the indigenous population moving out to better areas. What is possibly more important than this is the simple fact that immigration adds to an already acute housing problem in the U.K.

20. What are the likely economic consequences of the continuous growth of population in this country? (L)

The economic consequences of a growth in population vary according to the cause of such growth. There are four major causes of population growth. Firstly a decline in the death rate, secondly a rise in the birth rate, thirdly an increase in the rate of immigration or fourthly a decline in the rate of emigration. It is also obviously possible for the population to rise through a combination of such factors, but for the sake of discussion each will be examined individually.

The decline in the death rate has been one of the major causes of the rise in population in developed "western" countries for over a century. The economic consequences of this are that because of improved social conditions, medicine etc. average life expectancy has risen. This means that there are relatively a higher proportion of people in the retired (over 65) age group. Many such people continue to consume without adding to the production of the economy. They therefore represent a net consumption loss to the rest of society, or viewed differently the rest of society has to forego some consumption in order to keep many of the over sixty-five age group alive. This is, of course, looking at the problem from a strictly economic point of view, and in fact society, by its willing payments of old age pensions, appears perfectly willing to forego such consumption.

A second cause of a rise in population is a rise in birth rate. It was at one time thought that the demands of an industrial society would always maintain a high birth rate, as in the nineteenth century children's wages were a useful and in some cases vital supplement to family income. A rise in birth rate, ceteris paribus, will cause a rise in population which will tend to become numerically dominated by the young. The economic benefits, in terms of increased production, again may not be felt for some years in a modern western society where in the U.K., the school leaving age has recently been raised to sixteen and where nearly 15% of the 18-21 age group are in full time education, which takes over 7% of state expenditure. It may then take over twenty years for the economic effects of an increased birth rate to be felt by the rest of the population.

The third cause of increased population is a rise in the rate of immigration. The economic consequences to the receiving country of this depend on the type of immigration. In simple terms if the immigrant comes with his family it is likely that, even if he is gainfully employed, he may be a net drain on the receiving country's resources as the latter has to provide education for children, (possibly of a specialised nature) as well as possible income supplements. The single male immigrant however is more likely to make a net contribution to the receiving country as use of social capital (education, health facilities) is likely to be smaller and through the taxes that he pays he will make a net contribution.

The final cause of increased population is through a decline in the rate of emigration. This, to the U.K. for example, is likely to be beneficial as often in the past those who have emigrated have been highly skilled (brain-drain) which the country can ill-afford to lose. Some countries however benefit from emigration. In southern Italy, for example, high rates of emigration have meant that those left have been able to consolidate existing farms into larger units which have proved to be more efficient. Also temporary emigration has proved beneficial because the emigrant, on his return to his native land has been able to teach his countrymen the methods of production in use in the most advanced countries.

It should therefore be apparent that the economic consequences of population increase depend on the cause of the increase. However in recent years advanced countries have tried to reduce their rate of population increases for two main reasons. Firstly it has been argued that the world's food and raw materials supplies are being endangered by the rapid rate of population increase. Secondly in many developed countries, especially the U.K. there are severe congestion and environmental problems.

The economic consequences of an increased demand for food and raw materials through population increase means that, because supply is not infinite, the prices of such commodities are bound to rise. This would be particularly unfair on the less developed countries who would be unable to purchase essentials such as food with the possible consequence of mass starvation.

In the U.K. any further rises in population are likely to result in further congestion and reduction of countryside. Congestion occurs not only on roads but occurs in housing, with those who are able to afford to do so moving further and further away from the urban areas. Population growth also results in rapidly escalating prices of land with the consequent rise in the value of property.

Until fairly recently therefore it was assumed that a rise in population would probably result, given time, in a rise in GNP per head, which was thought to be an indication of improved welfare. Now however the attendant social costs associated with any increase in population such as congestion, despoilation of the environment probably dwarf any potential GNP growth benefits.

21. Outline the main changes in the size, age distribution and sex distribution of the population of the U.K. since 1945. Comment on the economic significance of the changes. (L)

There was no census of population between 1931 and 1951 and hence it is difficult to relate figures specifically to 1945. However it is not difficult to determine certain changes over the past 30 years. At the end of the war the total population of the U.K. was around 50 millions; currently it stands at around 56 millions. Although the population continues to increase, the rate of growth has declined in recent years.

There have also been considerable changes in the age distribution of the population. The most significant of these is increase in the proportion of the population over retiring age. Currently also the proportion of young people is relatively high.

The sex distribution has changed somewhat. Total births of boys exceed those of girls by about 6 per cent, but stillbirth rates and mortality rates at all ages are higher for males so that women outnumber men in the population as a whole and in all age groups over 45. Recently, the lengthening of the expectation of life, which has been rather more marked for women than for men, has increased the preponderance of women among the elderly – there are now some 19 women over 70 years old to every 10 men.

All these changes are economically significant. Any increase in the size of the population will increase overall demand. The pattern of demand will depend on which groups of the population have increased. It is suggested that the proportion of young people under 16 and the proportion of elderly people over 65 have both increased. Both these groups are dependent groups who have to be supported by the 16-65 age group. The relationship between these two groups combined and the working population is known as the "dependency ratio" which over the past thirty years has increased by some 50% and currently stands at over 650 dependents per thousand of the working population. The raising of the school leaving age and the decline in the birth and death rates have led to this increase in the dependent population. Because of this and the growing numbers of young people continuing in full time education, there is a special need to make the best use of national human resources, both by placing those available for work in suitable employment and by introducing technological improvements and wider training in order to raise productivity. An ageing population results in demand changes and can lead to structural unemployment. It also puts a far greater onus on the state social service and health provisions. Since changes in the sex distribution of the population have been most marked amongst the elderly some of the same economic effects apply.

Overall, as the proportion of dependents increases, major shifts in demand are likely to occur. The working population must be sufficiently skilled and mobile to meet this changing demand and its productivity must increase to counter the productivity lost by the young and the old.

22. Examine the ecnomic effects on a country of a large-scale emigration of young, working-age people without dependents. (L)

Young people of working age are clearly the part of the population that a country can least afford to lose. Prior to reaching working age, a person depends on the production of others for what he consumes. There are enormous demands upon the education and health services and the social services generally by people up to the age of sixteen. Additionally his parents have spent a good deal of money on him simply in the basic areas of food, clothing and shelter. For sixteen years he has been prepared to take his place as a user of goods or services. If at this stage – or very soon afterwards – he leaves the country permanently, the country has lost a good deal of production. The more that has been spent on him, the better the education he has had, the more sophisticated his preparation for a working life, the greater the loss will be. The phrase "brain drain' has been coined to try to give some idea of the adverse effect the emigration of a gifted person has upon his native country.

It could, of course, be argued that a person of working age emigrating spares his native country the task of maintaining him after retiring age. For emigrants within a few years of retirement, this might well be a valid point but it is not generally valid for the *young* worker.

From the economic point of view any person leaving the

country for good must represent a net loss if the expenditure upon him pre working age and post working age taken together exceeds the contribution he made during his working life.

Every producer is also a consumer, we might well be reminded. But, generally speaking, the consumption of young people of working age falls far below the contribution he makes to production.

We have, however, spoken of individuals and, to some extent, the economic effects of emigration depend on the degree to which the country from which the emigrants leave is over or under populated. There is, of course, the concept of the *optimum* population to be considered. This is broadly the most satisfactory population economically for a country. If a country is over-populated it might be that large scale emigration would enable it to reach its optimum and, in that sense, might be encouraged and be economically desirable. However, if the country concerned had very large proportions of very young and of old, the emigration on a large scale of young workers might make the problem worse – in this case perhaps it is large scale emigration of the more elderly workers that could assist. A country with an optimum population or a country under populated would certainly suffer enormously by the emigration of its producers.

23. Outline the distribution of the working population of the U.K. between various types of production (rough proportions only are required). Explain the reasons for this pattern and for recent changes in it. (L)

The total working population of the U.K. is approximately 25 millions. About 35 per cent of all employees work in manufacturing industries. Some 19 per cent are employed in financial, professional and scientific services (e.g. insurance, banking, education, medicine) and 12 per cent in the distributive trades. Just over 9 per cent work in miscellaneous services (including catering and hotels), 7 per cent in transport and communications and 7 per cent in public administration.

The construction industries account for nearly 6 per cent of all employees; agriculture, forestry and fishing for just under 2 per cent; mining and quarrying 1½ per cent; gas, electricity and water 1½ per cent.

These different industries can be grouped into primary, secondary and tertiary producers. Primary producers are those engaged in the extractive industries (agriculture, fishing, mining and quarrying) and in this broad group fall only some 3 per cent of the working population. Secondary producers are those engaged in manufacturing and construction industries and this accounts for over 40 per cent of the working population. Tertiary producers are those engaged in the service industries, in administration and in transport and together these account for between 50 and 60 per cent of the working population.

Over the past fifteen years there have been considerable changes in the occupational distribution of the population. The proportion of people working in extractive industries has continued to decline, the proportion of people working in tertiary production has continued to increase and the proportion working in secondary production has remained fairly steady although there have been significant changes within this large group.

It might well appear that the economy is well off balance if over half of the working population are engaged in tertiary production. However, the greater the degree of sophistication of a country, the higher its general standard of living, the greater the proportion of the population that will work in this sector of production. This sector of production includes health, education and the social services and the greater the degree of civilisation of a country the greater will be the demand for these services. This sector also deals with the leisure industries and with catering and these industries have expanded as the standard of living has risen.

The extractive industries have declined in importance especially with the introduction of new sources of power. But the decline in numbers is also partly due to technological factors and increased mechanisation.

In the manufacturing and construction industries, although the proportion employed in this sphere as a whole remains fairly constant, older industries have declined and newer ones taken their place and so there have been changes in the occupational distribution of the population within this sector.

Increased prosperity, automation, the growth of new industries are all factors that have affected the distribution of the working population between various types of production.

24. Explain the difference between structural unemployment and cyclical unemployment. (L)

Structural unemployment is a result of labour being out of line with industrial demand. Probably the best example of structural unemployment occurs when a geographical area producing a single product is affected by a permanent reduction in demand for that product. The industrial areas of the north of England and Scotland, for so long dependent on the textile, iron, coal and shipbuilding industries, all suffered badly in the inter-war years when demand for these products failed to keep pace with that for new science-based products. The resulting unemployment is known as structural unemployment. The ever-changing nature of the economy, the replacement of old techniques by new ones, the expansion and contraction of firms, the growth and decline in the importance of certain areas – all lead to unemployment of this nature. Structural unemployment calls for attempts to re-train employees and to mobilise labour in order to satisfy the voracious demands of a dynamic industrial society.

However, the fluctuations that have taken place in employment have not been confined to individual industries or regions. They have covered the whole field of industry in more or less regular oscillations – all, or nearly all, industries being simultaneously prosperous or depressed. There has been an alternation between boom and slump, the length of the cycle varying from six months to ten years. This alternation of boom and slump is known as the Trade Cycle and it is primarily an employment cycle. The main feature of a boom is a shortage of labour and the main feature of a slump is unemployment. This unemployment in times of slump is often referred to as cyclical unemployment. Its causes are rooted in the low level of demand for goods and services and the cure for such depressions must lie in increasing effective demand. This can be achieved by an increase in the government's own expenditure or by encouraging private investment or by encouraging consumption expenditure. The trade cycle, however, is really confined to one country at a time and any attempts to move from a slump to a boom must, of necessity, take into account the economic conditions prevailing in other parts of the world.

How to resolve the problem of cyclical unemployment remains one of the great imponderables of economics. Therefore it is the great unsolved question of economics, endlessly complicated, obscure and controversial.

25. What do you understand by "the mobility of labour"? To what extent do you think that unemployment is caused by low mobility of labour? (L)

"Mobility of labour" concerns the movement of members of the working population from one job to another job. Labour is the least mobile of the factors of production but the degree of immobility depends on the type of movement required. Sometimes the employee needs to move from one part of the country to the other; sometimes he needs simply to change employers whilst doing the same job as before; sometimes he needs to acquire a completely new skill.

Geographical mobility – moving from one part of the country to the other – is the most difficult. Very few people find moving about the country easy: it involves breaking long-established ties for oneself, one's wife and family and the older the employee the more difficult it is to face this movement. Additionally the expenses of moving and the finding of suitable, and suitably priced, accommodation create further problems.

Industrial mobility – moving from one employer to another whilst doing the same type of jobs – is probably easier than either geographical or occupational mobility (which involves changing skills). However, a natural conservatism, a reluctance to change the tried for the untried, a desire to remain with one's colleagues, a wish to keep to an established routine – all these factors militate against much industrial mobility. With wage differentials today at a minimum, this does not help the situation either.

Occupational mobility is almost as difficult as geographical mobility and the same factors militate against it as militate against industrial mobility. But there are, of course, added drawbacks to changing skills, drawbacks which – as with geographical mobility – are accentuated by age.

The relative immobility of labour certainly has some relationship to the numbers of unemployed. When large numbers are unemployed only a relatively small percentage are unemployed simply because of their comparative immobility. However, if the numbers of unemployed are much below half a million it is generally found that the number of unfilled vacancies exceeds the total number of unemployed and this, of course, can only really be explained in terms of the low mobility of labour – although, of course, there is always a certain amount of transitional unemployment (workers unemployed between jobs).

A good deal of unemployment in the U.K. is structural unemployment arising from the fact that the supply of labour is slow to adjust itself to major changes in the pattern of the economy. Following the Industrial Revolution, Britain's basic industries developed in certain areas but in this century this industrial structure and location became outdated. Since then a new generation of employees has entered the labour market and a good deal of Government assistance has been forthcoming to assist the growth and location of new industries. However, in the former prosperous areas and high industrial activity the percentage unemployed remains higher than in other areas indicating how immobile labour is. In this sense it does contribute to the problem of unemployment.

26. What is meant by regional policy? How can it contribute to the future economic development of the U.K.? (L)

Certain parts of Britain, mainly long-established centres of basic industries now losing their former importance, have for many years suffered higher than average levels of unemployment together with other signs of industrial decline such as high rates of outward migration and low levels of income per head, poor amenities and derelict buildings. The newer and expanding industries have tended to develop mostly in the Midlands and the South East, and unemployment has remained a persistent problem in Scotland, Wales, Northern Ireland and some parts of England, particularly the North and Merseyside. The ending of regional imbalance has been an objective of successive governments.

These areas of decline are designated Assisted Areas, and receive special help from the Government to enable them to overcome their particular social and economic problems. Broadly speaking these areas consist of Scotland, Wales, the North and North-West Regions, Yorkshire and Humberside, Cornwall, part of Devon, and parts of Nottinghamshire and Derbyshire. These areas have common problems, but suffer from them to different degrees, and are divided into three categories accordingly: Special Development Areas, where the problems are most acute, and Development Areas and Intermediate Areas where the problems are correspondingly less so. Government help is allocated among the three categories at appropriately varying levels.

This regional policy is aimed at redressing the balance between regions. The major economic justification for a regional policy is to obtain fuller utilisation of the country's resources in order to achieve a satisfactory rate of economic growth. Without some sort of regional policy there is bound to be a more than proportionate amount of unemployment in these assisted areas.

Differing levels of unemployment from region to region have effects on any policy to control inflation. In simple terms the problem is that unemployment can normally be reduced by an increase in effective demand, but if demand is set at too high a level this results in a strain on the labour force and consequently an increase in inflation. If therefore there is a variety of unemployment rates throughout the country then an increase in effective demand can result in a relatively minor reduction in unemployment in some areas but cause a considerable stimulus to inflation in others. Any regional policy aimed at reducing unemployment to a uniformly low level would assist the management of the economy and the future economic development of the United Kingdom.

Without a regional policy migration would occur from the development areas. This would mean that social capital – schools, hospitals – built for a population of a certain size would be underutilised. Moreover, the migration would result in further overutilisation of such capital in the areas to which the migrants would undoubtedly go. A regional policy can prevent this situation.

27. How may a government use fiscal policy to remove unemployment? (L)

In simple terms fiscal policy may be regarded as synonomous with taxation policy. In the U.K. taxes are both direct and indirect -- direct taxes being those on personal and corporate income such as income tax and indirect taxes being those levied on goods such as V.A.T. as well as duties on petrol, cigarettes and alcohol.

The level of taxation – both direct and indirect – is at the discretion of the Chancellor of the Exchequer and at Budget time (or through "mini-budgets" if the situation demands it) the Chancellor may reduce or increase these rates. If, for example, the economy is in need of the stimulus of general demand he may reduce the level of income tax. This means that the real income of individuals will rise and that they will in all probability spend this extra money. This raises the overall level of effective demand and to satisfy this more goods need to be produced. In many cases firms may take on more men, some of whom were previously unemployed. These men will have increased income which will be spent so raising further the level of effective demand. It will be recognised that this is the effect of the multiplier. Unfortunately, the present day multiplier is not large i.e. the effect just described continues for a relatively short time. Its ultimate effect is determined by the marginal propensity to save, to import, and to pay taxes i.e. an increase in any or all of these will reduce the effect of the multiplier.

Since 1945 much of the unemployment problem of the U.K. has been localised, particularly in the old industrial areas of Scotland, Northern England and South Wales. In some of these areas unemployment has been four times the national average at a time when inflation has been running at a high level. It is pointless, in these cases, for the Chancellor to reduce taxes and encourage spending since this only exacerbates the problem. Fiscal policy is therefore brought to bear specifically on the Assisted Areas. Cash grants to help towards capital expenditure on plant, machinery and buildings. Selective financial assistance is available under the Industry Act to encourage sound industrial projects which will improve employment prospects in the Assisted Areas. Such selective assistance takes the form of loans, interest relief grants and removal grants. In addition the Government has made available a regional employment premium, training assistance, help for transferred workers and contract preference schemes.

Ultimately the removal of unemployment depends on success in reducing the rate of inflation. Fiscal policies that can do this are bound also to reduce unemployment. Until inflation can be brought under control, fiscal policies can only check the rise in unemployment.

28. "Equal pay for equal work". Comment.

The concept of equal pay has come to the fore with the emancipation of women and especially through changes in the employment of men and women in the two wars. It is basically concerned that the recognised rate for a job shall be paid to any person who does it, or does a similar and comparable job, regardless of sex.

Jobs may be sorted out as sufficiently similar for the claim to apply by reference either to the labour grade or to the job content. In practice, very different jobs are not equated, and the claim is restricted to "similar employment", the degree of similarity being a matter of judgement in each case.

"Equal work" implies equality in the quantity of outputs as well as similarity in the kind of job. If any separable class of workers gets less done than others, they will not normally get employment at a common time rate. A common piece rate adjusts payments to outputs – but costs are higher for slower workers, and some may need special aids, hence the difference between gross and net outputs. Even when workers produce equal net output in similar jobs, they may differ in "overall value". A worker's overall value contains an allowance for his usefulness as a party to a long period association between firm and worker, and this depends on his versatility, reliability, trainability and promotability. In general, the wage-earner who expects to spend his life in a trade is more likely to be keen and willing to learn than one who expects to leave it before long.

In general, it can be said that there are perhaps four tests of "equal work" as a basis for "equal pay". Two workers may be deemed to have done equal work when, working in similar jobs, they have (1) worked for equal times, (2) turned out equal gross products, (3) turned out equal net products, and (4) satisfied one of the above *and* are fully interchangeable as parties to a long period association between wage-earner and firm.

Unequal pay arises as a consequence of differences in net output between employees and differences in overall value. As far as net output is concerned, where output depends upon bodily strength, for example, some groups of workers are clearly less efficient than others. Differences in overall value depend upon a number of factors e.g. how long, all other things being equal, the employee is likely to remain in the employers employment.

The whole concept of equal pay for equal work really turns on what constitutes equal work and the difficulties involved in measuring this.

29. Compare the economic effects of basing the distribution of income on (a) the needs of individual members of the community and (b) the productivity of the resources owned by individual members.

We are concerned here with the contrast between personal incomes based on need and personal incomes based on factor prices. "Needs" must be defined. Some people regard "needs" as just sufficient to keep them alive; others regard "needs" as that which will maintain a certain standard of life, according to occupation; yet others regard "needs" as that which enables them to live comfortably (whatever that itself may mean). However defined, needs vary from individual to individual. A growing young man requires more food than an aged lady; the aged lady requires different food from the young man. A professor requires a different "uniform" from a coal miner. A doctor needs a car, an artist needs pens, pencils, boards etc. Needs vary according to age, sex, occupation, social standing and other related factors. This difficulty in accurately defining needs and the recognition that needs vary considerably means that any attempt to base the distribution of income on individual needs would result in some people being dissatisfied since their "needs" would have been inaccurately defined. Such dissatisfaction would affect output.

Distributing income according to needs would also necessarily involve a good deal of central control which, to a large extent, is impracticable.

It could be argued that distribution of income according to need would encourage maximum output since presumably all employees would be highly satisfied. However this income has to be produced in the first place and incentives are needed to encourage people to learn skills and to work to maximum capacity. Such incentives must be measured in monetary terms and rewarded by money payments. But with income distributed according to need this would not be possible. Yet without these incentives, why should people work at all? Clearly this would affect output unless acceptable non-economic incentives could be found. In "Modern Capitalism and Economic Progress", Thomas Wilson notes that "in the end, the attempt to divorce incomes from the value of the work done would result in frustration and defeat. It would imply dictatorship and that in turn implies privilege and inequality". Clearly the practical objective is a kind of compromise between distribution of income that is required for *efficiency* and that which is required for *equity*.

A system of distribution of income according to the productivity of the resources owned by the individual members at least means that land, labour and capital are more likely to be used in an economically desirable fashion than if individual needs were the sole determinant. Interest is high where capital is most needed, rent is high where sites are most economical by demand, wages are high where labour has a scarcity value. As yet, the economic system has not yet devised anything to replace the price mechanism which is essentially based on demand and supply and if income is distributed in the same way this is probably the most economically efficient way. As far as labour is concerned, the greatest difficulty is in measuring productivity – especially of employees in the service industries.

30. Describe and account for the relative decline in the U.K. manufacturing industry.

Over the past ten years there has been a continuing upward trend in manufacturing output by volume, though this is modified, as would be expected, by cyclical fluctuations. It has, however, grown at a pace slower than in many of the other major industrial countries with whom we have to compete, and has been associated with a gradual decline in the manufacturing industry's share of total output. Such falls have also occurred in other countries e.g. France, West Germany and U.S.A., but they have been less pronounced; in some major countries (e.g. Japan and Italy) the proportion taken by manufacturing industry has actually increased.

Between 1964 and 1974 there has been a steady drift downwards in employment in the manufacturing sector, amounting to over ½ million over the whole ten years. The process has been slow on the whole; over this period manufacturing's share fell from 37 per cent to 35 per cent. Over the same period there was a very slight fall in total numbers of employees in employment. The shift out of manufacturing has been accompanied by a rise in the numbers of employees in service industries and many parts of the public sector. Meanwhile in other countries manufacturing employment has been increasing.

Several instances have been cited publicly of significant absolute productivity differences between factories in Britain and similar factories abroad but Britain's recent record (from about 1971) of growth in productivity has been broadly in line with that of some other major industrial countries, though far outstripped by one or two others. Where Britain compares less well is in keeping up the impetus of growth in output as a whole. For example, in 1968-73 output in West Germany rose 33 per cent and productivity (output per man-hour) 28 per cent compared to 15 per cent and 23 per cent in the U.K. In other words in the U.K. output has grown more slowly than productivity – hence the fall in employment – whereas in other countries it has kept pace with productivity growth so that employment in industry has been maintained.

The annual volume of gross U.K. manufacturing investment increased by over 30 per cent between 1964 and 1974. However, the level fluctuates sharply in accordance with the course of the business cycle, and this figure therefore conceals several more or less violent changes of direction within the period. Overall, most of the other leading countries have grown – in terms of manufacturing investment, at a faster rate than U.K. In terms of the proportion of GDP spent on manufacturing investment U.K. comes off very badly in comparison with other leading countries.

In terms of capital stock in manufacturing in relation to the labour force, the capital-labour ratio has increased. In recent years there has been a steady rise in capital stock taken in combination with a reducing labour force. Employment per unit of output has fallen and capital per unit of output has been rising.

Britain is more dependent on its export trade than many other developed countries. It has, however, been less successful in holding on to its position in world trade. Over many years the share of manufactured goods in Britain's exports has remained at the high level of 80 per cent. But Britain has not succeeded in keeping or extending its share of world export markets for manufactured goods. This share has steadily diminished. Meanwhile imports of manufactured goods have made increasing inroads into the domestic market. Traditionally Britain has been an importer mainly of raw materials and foodstuffs, and an exporter of manufactures, but now over half of our imports consist of manufactured goods.

31. Describe the main categories of government expenditure in the United Kingdom. What forces have determined the size of each category? (L)

Government expenditure is reviewed annually and the results published in a Government White Paper, "Public Expenditure". Vast sums of money are involved and in 1975/76 some £43,000 million was budgeted for expenditure on public services. This sum represents a substantial part of the nation's total resources.

The largest category of government expenditure is pensions and other social security benefits, currently accounting for some 18% of all government expenditure. For a number of years this category has taken an increasing proportion of public monies. Public expenditure on social security now averages £125 per year for each man, women and child in the country. It has increased as the scope of social security has increased and as the level of benefits has progressively increased. The government provides a comprehensive system of social security, comprising national insurance, industrial injuries insurance, family allowances, family income supplements, supplementary benefits, war pensions and other benefits. Nowadays, most people receive social security benefits of one sort or another at some stage in their lives. Retirement pensions are the largest single item and account for about half the expenditure. There are now some 8 million people receiving national insurance retirement benefits and this number is increasing. This, coupled with the fact that expenditure on pensions and other long-term benefits will continue to grow in real terms as they will in future be increased in line with earnings, means that this category of government expenditure is likely to take an even larger share of the national cake.

Education is another main category of government expenditure accounting for about 12p in the pound of all public spending. It averages in the region of £400 a year for every pupil and student. The percentage of government expenditure going on education is likely to be maintained as more and more places become available for the under-fives and as the continuing programme for the replacement and improvement of old schools goes ahead. Education has been responsible for such a large proportion of public spending as standards over the years have been improved and as equal opportunity has gradually become something of a reality. Furthermore, the demands of the second half of the twentieth century are for educated, trained, skilled and professional workers more than ever before.

Health and the personal social services form the third most important cateogry taking 10% of government spending. Health and personal social services are provided, for the most part free of charge, for the whole population. Here again as standards have improved and as the scope of these services has widened, so the proportion of public expenditure on them has increased. Care for the elderly in all its forms is an essential part of these personal social services and an ageing population necessarily results in more expenditure on these services.

Defence accounts for some 9% of government spending whereas in the late 1960s it was taking some 16%. The proportion spent on defence has been declining as our commitments in this direction have decreased.

Housing takes a similar percentage of public money and this sum has mainly assisted those buying their own homes since the expenditure on providing most rented accommodation is met by local authorities. Most owner-occupiers get tax allowances to set against the interest payments on their mortgages. People whose incomes are too low for them to pay much tax can benefit instead from the option mortgage scheme, which reduces the rate of interest they have to pay when they buy a home. This, together with a greater number of owner-occupiers in recent years, has meant that expenditure on housing by the government has been high.

Commerce, industry and agriculture likewise account for another 9% of government spending. Food subsidies, expenditure on agricultural price guarantees and grants and aid to industry have all meant considerable government expenditure.

Debt interest, nationalised industries' investment, and roads and transport are three other important categories of government expenditure.

As the standard of living of a country increases, as a country gradually assumes more and more of a social conscience, government expenditure increases. Since 1945 there have been vast areas which previously were neglected or where the citizen had to have the money to benefit, which now come within the orbit of the state and this has necessarily resulted in a high level of government spending.

32. What are the relative merits and demerits of direct and indirect taxation? (S)

Direct taxes are those which are imposed on the person who is intended to bear the ultimate loss e.g. income tax. The revenue from such taxes goes direct to the authority (usually the central government) levying the taxes.

Indirect taxes, on the other hand, are those whose burden is intended to be shifted in some way. For example, V.A.T. is such a tax. Taxes on commodities are always indirect for the consumer usually bears the greater part of the burden (as he was meant to do) but the dealer must pay the tax in the first place. The revenue from such taxes usually therefore goes *indirectly* to the authority (usually the central government again) levying the taxes.

A system of direct taxation possesses many advantages. The incidence (i.e. who ultimately pays?) is easier to determine and hence the tax can be made to fall upon those on whom it is intended to fall. Direct taxation can also be progressive i.e. as one's income increases, the percentage taken in taxation increases. Furthermore an increase in national income automatically yields an increase in tax revenue. It also enables the state to reach people who make a living in one country but live for part of the year in another. Within reasonable limits direct taxation is elastic which is another advantage. Direct taxation also possesses the merit of being relatively easy and cheap to collect and also allows the taxpayer to know exactly how much he is paying.

The demerits of a system of direct taxation occur mainly in the method of administration and are relatively insignificant compared to the advantages. There is more possibility of evasion in direct than in indirect taxation but with increasing efficiency and sophistication in the field of collection there is comparatively little evasion. Direct taxation is inconvenient to the taxpayer since it requires the completion of complicated forms and hence compares adversely with the simplicity of indirect taxation for the taxpayer. Moreover, many people prefer to be "taxed in the dark" i.e. to have the tax concealed in the price of an article rather than to have it made brutally clear what they are paying.

Indirect taxation obviously counters the disadvantages of direct taxation mentioned above: evasion is difficult, collection is comparatively easy (each individual practically taxes himself) and the taxpayer does not feel the burden so heavily since it is spread over a number of purchases throughout the year and is mainly hidden from view. It possesses more important merits than these however. A system of indirect taxation allows those with small incomes to be reached and also enables the state to extract revenue from foreign visitors who otherwise would be exempt from taxation. It means also that a tax on luxuries falls on the incomes of the relatively wealthy. Furthermore, it is to a certain extent elastic according to the elasticity of demand for the taxed commodity. Indirect taxation can also be used by governments to check the consumption of an undesirable commodity (at least as far as those on lower incomes are concerned) and to cut back demand for certain products.

The outstanding disadvantage of indirect taxation is that it is usually regressive in character since as one's income increases the percentage taken in indirect taxation appreciably diminishes. If the tax is "specific" (i.e. a flat rate on all grades of the commodity) and not "ad valorem" (i.e. according to the value of each grade of the commodity) it is doubly regressive because in proportion to the price paid the tax on the lower priced articles is a greater burden. A person on a low income who regards tea as a necessity will be more heavily taxed if tea is taxed than a person on a high income who might use wine instead. Moreover, if the tax on tea is a flat rate of 10p per half kilo the family purchasing cheap tea is paying more heavily than the family purchasing dear tea. Apart from its regressive nature, the incidence (i.e. who ultimately pays?) is not always easy to determine – the government obtains its income but it cannot be certain from which sections that income has come. The revenue from indirect taxation is always uncertain unless the demand for the commodity taxed is inelastic. Indirect taxation can be harmful to industry especially when levied on a producer's good. It suffers also from the fact that it is comparatively expensive to the state: though collection itself is easy the costs of collection and of avoiding fraud, are often heavy.

Since there are so many merits and demerits of each system, it is not surprising that most governments use a combiation of the two systems to raise revenue.

33. Show how local government spending is financed.

The whole system of local authority expenditure and finance is currently under review by the advisory committee under the Chairmanship of Mr. Frank Layfield. Their report is expected shortly but the system of finance currently pertaining is outlined here.

Current revenue is roughly £10,000 million (£9,845 million in 1945). It consists of three major elements – rates (£2,971 million in 1974), grants from central government (£4,779 million in 1974) and other income (£2,011 million in 1974).

Rates are the only local tax. They are levied on occupiers of property (certain classes of property, however – notably agricultural land and buildings – are exempt). Each occupier pays annually the product of (i) the rateable value of the property and (ii) the rate poundage fixed for the year by the local authority. *Rateable Value* is broadly equivalent to annual rental value, as assessed, in England and Wales, by the Inland Revenue Department, and in Scotland, by special assessors. The *rate poundage* is in effect the local tax rate – the amount per pound of rateable value the occupier is asked to pay. Not all ratepayers however pay the full rate poundage. Householders pay at a lower rate poundage than non-domestic ratepayers. Reliefs also apply to charities, to certain non-profit making bodies and, in Scotland, to industry and freight transport, but in these cases the cost is not recoverable from central government. Finally, rebates are made to impecunious householders.

Grants are of two main kinds: specific and supplementary grants paid towards expenditure on specified services (around £700 million in 1974) and rate support grants paid as general grants in aid of revenue (over £4,000 million in 1974).

The Government fixes the *national total* of the rate support grants (RSG) and other revenue grants according to the view it takes of the respective shares of the cost of local services that ought to be borne directly by ratepayers on the one hand and by central taxation on the other. The RSG total is divided into three different "elements", and these are shared out between local authorities as follows:

(a) the 'needs element' – to compensate for differences between authorities in the amounts they need to spend on their services (arising from such factors as differences from area to area in the number of school-children to be educated).
(b) the 'resources element' – to compensate for differences between authorities in their tax-raising capacity, in terms of the total amount of rateable value they have in proportion to their population.
(c) the 'domestic element' – to meet the cost to the authorities of domestic rate relief.

The main items in other local authority income are rents from council housing (£1,200 million in 1974), rent from other land and buildings (£500 million in 1974) and service of debt to the local authorities, mainly mortgage interest and repayments (£300 million in 1974).

Capital revenue runs at roughly £4,000 million (£3,986 million in 1974) and the largest element here is borrowing from external sources (some £1,265 million from central government and some £2,075 million other identified borrowing in 1974), compared with £720 million in 1974 provided by internal financing (surplus of current revenue over current expenditure).

34. In what aspects has there been a change in the U.K. standard of living over the past fifty years?

It has been customary, until the very recent past, to assume that the standard of living during the past fifty years in the U.K. has risen almost continuously. It has always been recognised that standards may have fallen during the 1930's at times of high unemployment in Northern England, Central Scotland and South Wales, but even then the standard of living for those actually in work probably rose quite substantially. However it has now become "fashionable" to suggest that in recent years the standard of living may also have fallen through factors such as greater pressures and strain in everyday life, damage to the environment, and overcrowding.

This illustrates the difficulty of measuring standards of living. In past years changes in the level of gross national product (GNP) per head has been taken as indicative of the standard of living but it has become increasingly unrealistic to use this measure. It only includes the acquisition of physical possessions such as motor cars, and televisions but it does not include such matters as increased leisure, reduced infant mortality, and lower rates of unemployment.

It is probably easiest to deal firstly with those factors which have resulted in an increase in the standard of living. In the first place economic growth of GNP in U.K. has, over the last fifty years, been higher than for any other comparative period in history – even at the time of the so called "Industrial Revolution". (The fact that during these fifty years other countries have grown faster should not however be forgotten.) Even allowing for the effect of inflation "real" National Product has risen at an unparalleled rate – an average of 2.9% for the past twenty years and 2.2% for the period 1922-1939 – though of course there are considerable year to year fluctuations in growth rates. Economic growth has meant that more goods could be purchased by individuals, provided that there was no evidence of this extra purchasing power being concentrated in the hands of a few. In fact the opposite has occurred. With the increasing importance of the government as an economic unit more money has been collected in taxes which in some cases were sharply progressive. This has meant a substantial redistribution of income since 1945 with the 'Gini' coefficients having fallen by 10% during the period, so that there are reduced proportions of the population which can be classified as either very rich or very poor in terms of income.

Over the past fifty years the standard of living has also been improved for most people by the lower levels of unemployment and the introduction of the welfare state which, among other things, has cushioned the effect of unemployment on those unfortunate enough to be in that position. Certainly since the Beveridge proposals of 1945 and Keynsian management of the economy, unemployment has rarely risen above a national average of 4%, and even in the worst affected regions, rates have rarely exceeded 8%-10%. This contrasts strongly with the years 1930-32 when there was an average of 16.8% of the labour force unemployed – though it should not be imagined that this was a typical pre 1945 decade. In the period 1860-1900 unemployment rates are calculated as being little over 4% – though there may have been considerable disguised underemployment in agriculture at that time.

It is often assumed that man has the basic needs for food, clothing and shelter. As a result of economic growth, reduced unemployment and a more equitable distribution of income, he has been able to purchase both better and more food and clothing. The housing situation has also improved considerably. In 1966 over 47% of households owned their own houses. In the 1920's this proportion would have been under 20%. Much of the improvements in housing standards have occurred since 1945. For example in 1951 52% of households had exclusive use of basic domestic amenities, but by 1966 this had risen to 73%. The proportions of houses having their own bathrooms or water closets has also increased substantially.

Finally there is every evidence of the increased health of the population. Infant mortality has fallen almost continously since the turn of the century. The average life expectancy has risen to over seventy years and many diseases which previously contributed substantially to the death rate are now curable provided they are detected at a sufficiently early stage. The National Health Service ensures that even the poorest person can obtain treatment in a hospital at little cost to himself.

This relatively glowing picture should not be allowed to gloss over those aspects which suggest that though the standard of living may have increased, the quality of life may not have risen proportionately. Thus, though the average number of hours worked has undoubtedly fallen the time spent travelling to work has undoubtedly increased. Though there has certainly been an improvement in housing generally between 1961 and 1966 the number of households in shared dwellings actually increased by 30%. Equally, though people are housed with more amenities such as bathrooms they often are in tower blocks of flats where they may be lonely and where mothers are constantly concerned for the safety of their children. There can be no doubt that there has been a reduction in unemployment since the gloomy days of the 1930's. Nevertheless the automated processes of production may result in monotonous and repetitive work for operatives and this is often cited as at least part cause of industrial strife and social unrest. Finally, though it is suggested that we are presently living in a "golden age" it is thought that excessive concern with the production of consumer goods and rapid population rise is destroying the natural environment. It is argued that the quality of life is being destroyed by sprawling urbanisation, by noise from aircraft and motor vehicles, by pollution of the air, river and seas by chemicals which are by-products of the industrial processes. There are fewer places where man can go for the peace and solitude that was a feature of pre-industrial society.

In conclusion it is difficult to ignore such powerful environmental arguments despite the difficulties of quantifying them. There can however be little doubt that the standard of living has increased but certainly by less than the amounts that a simple study of GNP growth would suggest.

35. Explain what is meant by marginal, average and total costs. Should a firm close down if it cannot cover its average costs? (L)

Total cost is the full cost of producing a level of output. It is important to note that this does not include any costs to the community either through, for example, pollution, or subsidy, but simply those costs which the firm incurs. Generally speaking, total costs increase with output. Total costs, of course, include both fixed costs and variable costs.

Average cost is simply total cost divided by output. Average costs therefore include both fixed and variable costs. They represent the average cost of producing one unit of output.

Marginal cost also derives from the concept of total costs. It is the increase in total costs deriving from the smallest possible increase in output. If the total costs of producing 9 units of output is £104,000 and the total cost of producing 10 units of output is £117,000 then the marginal cost of the 10th unit is £117,000 – £104,000, i.e. £13,000.

A business man will continue to incur costs as long as his marginal costs (the costs of producing an additional unit of output) do not exceed his marginal revenue (the revenue derived from the sale of an additional unit of output), and he will continue to increase his output as long as this difference exists. The extent of the supply that is forthcoming is dependent, therefore, on the relation between marginal cost and marginal revenue. The last unit a producer will be induced to supply at existing prices is the marginal unit i.e. that unit the costs of which are just covered by the additional revenue received.

In the long run a firm must cover all its costs (including some profit) i.e. the average cost must not exceed average revenue. If over the long period it cannot cover average costs a firm will be forced to close down. Before doing so, however, it would have to review its production methods, its administrative machinery, its pricing policy, its marketing and numerous other factors in order to attempt to reduce costs.

In the short run a firm may well be operating at a loss from time to time and not covering its average costs. Here a distinction between fixed and variable costs is useful. Revenue from present sales might well not cover the fixed costs but might exceed the variable costs. In this case there would be a net gain for the time being in continuing production.

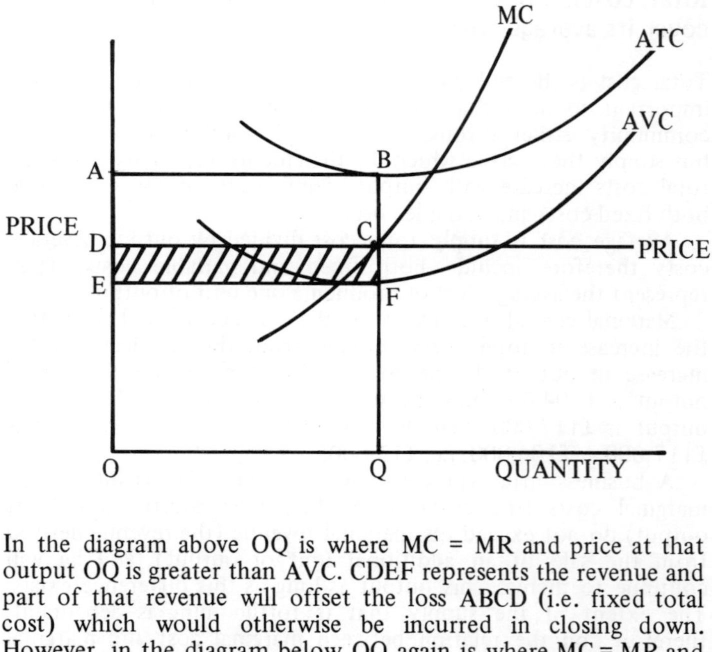

In the diagram above OQ is where MC = MR and price at that output OQ is greater than AVC. CDEF represents the revenue and part of that revenue will offset the loss ABCD (i.e. fixed total cost) which would otherwise be incurred in closing down. However, in the diagram below OQ again is where MC = MR and price at output OQ is less than AVC. Here it can be seen that CDEF is a further loss incurred by continuing production in addition to the loss ABCD. In this case the firm ought to close down forthwith.

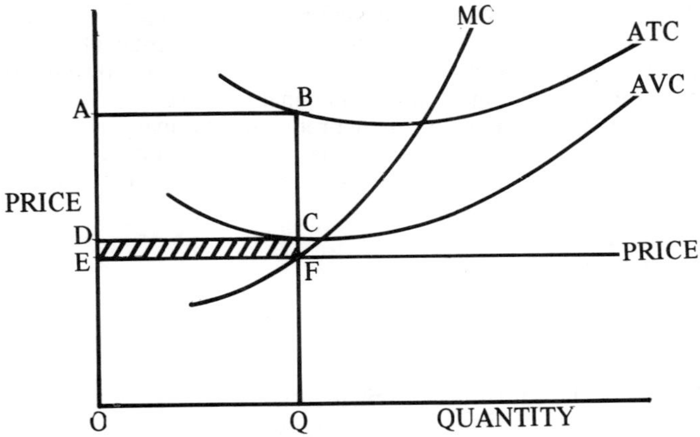

36. What do you understand by the terms marginal revenue and marginal cost? Explain the role of these concepts in the theory of the firm. (L)

The extent to which a firm can expand or contract output depends on the relationship between marginal cost and marginal revenue. Marginal revenue is, therefore, of some importance in determining the extent of output.

Revenue is distinct from profit. Revenue is the total receipts from the sale of goods; profit is the difference between revenue and costs. Marginal revenue is the addition to total receipts resulting from the sale of the marginal addition to output. The demand schedule for commodity Z is

Quantity	*Price*
1	12
2	10
3	7
4	3

To this can be added the total revenue column and a marginal revenue column:

Quantity	*Price*	*Total Revenue*	*Marginal Revenue*
1	12	12	12
2	10	20	8
3	7	21	1
4	3	12	–9

This shows us that the additional revenue obtained by producing 2 units instead of 1 is 8; the additional revenue obtained by producing 3 units instead of 2 is 1. This additional revenue from the sale of the marginal unit is marginal revenue.

Marginal cost is the cost of producing the marginal unit. It is the addition to total costs that an additional unit of production makes. For commodity Z the total costs might be as follows:

Quantity	*Total Cost*
1	20
2	29
3	30
4	32

To this can be added the marginal cost:-

Quantity	*Total Cost*	*Marginal Cost*
1	20	20
2	29	9
3	30	1
4	32	2

This shows that the additional costs incurred in increasing production from 1 unit to 2 units is 9; in increasing production from 2 units to 3 units is 1. This addition to costs resulting from the production of the marginal unit is marginal cost.

These two concepts together play an important part in the theory of the firm. They are the key to deciding what is the firm's most profitable output, whether it is operating in a perfect or imperfect market. Generally speaking, in the short run it must pay a firm to keep increasing its production while marginal revenue exeeds marginal cost, but to stop increasing production before marginal cost exceeds marginal revenue. The best and most profitable output is where marginal revenue and marginal cost are equal. In the example of commodity Z above, marginal revenue equals marginal cost at 3 units of production. As long as revenue increases more than costs, production will be extended. A producer will continue to expand his output as long as the increase in total costs is less than the increase in total revenue. He will contract his output if marginal costs exceed marginal revenue, and he will expand output if marginal revenue exceeds marginal cost. When marginal revenue and marginal cost are equal, any change in output, either by expansion or by contraction, will reduce profits.

In conditions of perfect competition, marginal revenue is equal to price, but the same principle, that output is extended to the point where marginal revenue and marginal cost are equal, still applies. In such conditions, marginal cost equals price.

37. Costs and revenue of firm X per week:

Output (units)	*Total Costs (£000's)*	*Total Revenue (£000's)*
4	47	76
5	57	90
6	66	102
7	74	112
8	80	120
9	85	126
10	91	130
11	99	132
12	110	132

(assume for all parts of the question that only whole units can be produced.)

(a) What output per week would maximise Firm X's profits?

(b) What is the marginal cost of producing 10 units of output?

(c) What would be the effect on output of levying on firm X a lump sum tax of (i) £40,000, (ii) £45,000?

(d) Suppose that in a no tax situation the firm were offered £100,000 to produce 5 units per week for a special customer; that the cost situation is still as specified in the schedule and that any further output can be sold on the market as indicated by the revenue schedule. Should the contract be accepted? What, if any, additional output would be sold and at what price? (L)

(a) Profits are maximised at the output at which the greatest total profit is made. The profit, when output is 9 units, is £41,000 and this is the greatest profit made at the given outputs. Hence 9 units is the weekly output which would maximise Firm X's profits.

(b) Marginal cost of producing 10 units of output is the difference in total costs when producing 10 units as compared to producing 9 units. Total cost of 10 units = £91,000 and total cost of 9 units = £85,000. Hence marginal cost of producing 10 units = £91,000 – £85,000 = £6,000.

(c) (i) A lump sum tax of £40,000 would add £40,000 to the total costs at all outputs and the only output that any profit at all would be made at existing prices would be 9 units again. Here profit would be £1,000 per week and at all other outputs no profit would be made.

(ii) A lump sum tax of £45,000 would mean that there will be no ouptut at which total revenue exceeds total costs i.e. a loss will be made whatever the level of output. If the firm could foresee this situation it would go out of business rather than incur this tax. If it could not foresee the situation it would continue in production in the short run, provided it could cover variable costs.

(d) To answer this it is necessary to consider Average Revenue at each output. Then assuming the first five units of output are sold for £100,000, the remaining units will be sold at Average Revenue price and total revenue can be calculated.

Output (*Units*)	*Total Costs* (*£000s*)	*Av. Rev.* (*i.e. Total Rev ÷ Output*) (*£000s*)	*Total Rev. (inc. special order)* (*£000s*)
4	47	19	
5	57	18	100
6	66	17	117
7	74	16	132
8	80	15	145
9	85	14	156
10	91	13	165
11	99	12	172
12	110	11	177

The profit maximising output is 10 units because here total profit is £74,000 – greater than that at any other output. He should accept the contract since previously his maximum possible profit was only £41,000. He would sell 5 further units of output at £13,000 per unit.

38. Define the multiplier. How is it related to the marginal propensity to consume? (L)

An increase in investment will result in an increase in the national income greater than the initial investment. The ratio of the eventual effect to the initial investment is defined as the multiplier.

Leaving aside international trade, the size of the multiplier depends upon what proportion of an increase in their incomes people decide to spend (the "propensity to consume") and upon what proportion they save (the "propensity to save"). Since all income must be spent or saved, the propensity to consume and the propensity to save must always equal one. In practice these proportions change as income changes so that in considering the effect of any change in the investment on the level of national income one is always concerned with the *marginal* propensity to consume (MPC) which tends to fall as income increases, and the *marginal* propensity to save (MPS) which tends to rise as income increases.

Let us suppose that the government decides to spend an extra £100 million on the shipbuilding industry. This £100 million will be the total amount by which the incomes of those concerned in this new project with rise. It will be paid as wages and salaries, profits, rents and so on. If the marginal propensity to consume is ¾ they will spend £75 million out of this £100 million. This £75 million becomes £75 additional expenditure of which a further ¾ provides yet more additional expenditure (¾ of £75 million, in this case, i.e. £56 million). This process continues until total incomes have increased by £400 million or four times the original government investment. The multiplier is 4. It will always be the reciprocal of the marginal propensity to save.

In the example it has been assumed that no international trade takes place and that no government taxation is imposed. Both imports and taxation forcibly raise the MPS. These are known as "leakages" and result in a lower value for the multipler.

Expressed as an equation where K = multiplier, r = MPC, s = MPS, in a closed economy without international trade or taxation

$$K = \frac{1}{1-r} = \frac{1}{s}$$

Having regard to international trade and taxation and with m = proportion spent on imports and t = proportion used in taxation

$$K = \frac{1}{s+m+t}$$

39. An imaginary economy is in equilibrium with no foreign trade or government activity. The *average propensity to consume* and the *marginal propensity to consume* are both 8/10, the actual level of consumption expenditure being £16,000 in each year.

(a) Explain the italicized phrases.

(b) What is the level of investment expenditure each year?

(c) What is the value of the multiplier?

Suppose that with investment expenditure unchanged both average and marginal propensities to consume drop to ¾.

(d) What will be the new equilibrium level of national income?

(e) Explain *briefly* the effects on the equilibrium of this simple system, by introducing foreign trade and government activity. (L)

(a) The propensity to consume represents that proportion of income which is spent. The proportion of income spent is not constant, however, at very low levels of income people will even draw on their savings and spending on consumption will actually exceed income. At high levels of income the proportion of income spent falls. The average propensity to consume is the mathematical average of these. The marginal propensity to consume relates to the proportion of *additional* income that people spend.

(b) If consumption expenditure is £16,000 and this represents an MPC of 8/10 then £16000 = 8/10 of investment injected. Hence the investment injected = £20,000. But 2/10 (i.e. £4,000) is investment expenditure.

(c) As MPC = 8/10 then MPS = 2/10 and the multiplier must be the reciprocal of the latter i.e. 10/2 i.e. 5.

(d) If MPC = ¾ then MPS = ¼. But this ¼ represents £4,000 since investment expenditure (i.e. amount saved) is unchanged. Hence the new equilibrium level of national income must be £16,000 (i.e. 4 x £4,000).

(e) Foreign trade would result in importing of goods and government activity would result in taxation. These represent leakages in the system and the value of the multiplier would fall and the increase in national income resulting from an injection of investment will be lower than if there were no international trade or government activity. However, both international trade and government activity have reverse sides in the form of exports and government expenditure which represent further injections.

APPENDIX I

The University of London have introduced a new Paper 3 in Economics at Advanced Level which will be examined for the first time in June 1977. Candidates are required to answer three questions out of five in one and three quarter hours (the first fifteen minutes of which should be spent in reading the paper). The University of London have issued five specimen questions which are reproduced below by kind permission of the University of London University Entrance and School Examinations Council. The specimen answers have also been provided by the University of London but they should not be regarded as model or ideal answers, but rather as the type of answer that one might expect from a better than average candidate, one who identifies the main issues in the various questions.

SPECIMEN PAPER 75/76 **APRIL 1975**

This specimen paper illustrates the new Paper 3 in Economics at Advanced Level, which will be examined for the first time in June 1977. Specimen answers are given.

UNIVERSITY OF LONDON

General Certificate of Education Examination

JUNE 1977 **ADVANCED LEVEL**

Subject Title	**Economics**
Paper No./Title	Paper 3
Subject Code No.	120

One and three quarter hours

Answer ANY THREE questions.
All questions carry equal marks.
Candidates are advised to spend the first fifteen minutes reading the paper.
Candidates are reminded of the necessity for good English and orderly presentation in their answers.

Turn over

PSE75/1111NS 3/12500

1. A group of market gardeners had for many years sent their tomatoes to be sold at the weekly market in Littledale. However, the Littledale Council decided to ban street car parking near the market with the result that the number of people shopping in the market decreased substantially. At first the farmers continued to send their tomatoes to the Littledale market in the hope that trade might pick up again. However, those farmers living furthest away eventually switched their supplies to Fullbrook where conditions for shopping were more favourable.

Show, by means of one diagram, the demand and supply conditions at Littledale:

(a) before the parking ban was introduced;
(b) immediately after the parking ban was introduced;
(c) after some supplies had been switched to Fullbrook.

Explain your diagram with a few sentences.

2. Below are estimates of the allocation of income from (i) employment and (ii) profits, which accounted for 63% and 37% respectively of total national income.

(i) *Allocation of income from employment* (= 63%)

Tax on employment income	13	
Disposable income from employment		50
Personal savings	7	
Spent on consumption at market prices		43
Of which: expenditure taxes	7	
imports	9	
Spent on domestic consumption at factor cost	27	
	63	

(ii) *Allocation of income from profits* (= 37%)

Tax on profits	14	
Profits after tax		23
Retained profits	11	
Distributed in dividends		12
Tax on dividends	5	
Private disposable income from profits		7
Personal savings	2	
Spent on consumption at market prices		5
Of which: expenditure taxes	1	
imports	1	
Spent on domestic consumption at factor costs	3	
	37	

(a) Assuming that additional income would be allocated as above, calculate the value of the multiplier.
(b) Discuss, with particular reference to the above data, the determinants of the multiplier.

3.

Output per year	Total cost (£000s)	Total revenue (£000s)
0	15	0
..	..	..
..	..	..
..	..	..
4	55	88
5	65	108
6	75	120
7	85	133
8	95	144
9	105	150
10	115	158

(a) On the basis of the above cost and revenue schedules, find the profit maximising output. (Assume that only complete units can be made.)
(b) What would be the profit maximising output if the firm had to install additional equipment which increased fixed costs by
 (i) £10,000 a year?
 (ii) £60,000 a year?

Turn over

4. Index of Industrial Production 1970. (1963 = 100)

Total all industries	124
Mining and quarrying	78
Manufacturing: total	127
Food, drink and tobacco	122
Coal and petroleum	151
Chemicals and allied industries	158
Metal manufacture	115
Instrument engineering	135
Electrical engineering	149
Shipbuilding	86
Vehicles (including aircraft)	116
Textiles	125
Leather, leather goods, fur	93
Clothing and footwear	103
Bricks, pottery, glass, cement	125
Timber, furniture	114
Paper, printing, publishing	121
Construction	116
Gas, electricity, water	144

Identify the major changes in industrial production that have occurred since 1963 and discuss the factors which have been mainly responsible for these changes.

5. *Unemployment, January 1972*

	Number unemployed (000s)	*% of total employees*
Development Areas (Incl. SDAs):		
Scottish	144,170	7.5
South Western	9,997	7.3
Merseyside	54,843	6.9
Northern	93,351	6.8
Welsh	40,011	6.3
All Development Areas	342,372	7.0
Northern Ireland	46,045	8.9
All Intermediate Areas	80,483	5.6
Great Britain	997,600	4.3

What light do the above figures throw on the success of the government's regional policies?
What additional information would you find useful in attempting to evaluate these policies?

UNIVERSITY OF LONDON
General Certificate of Education Examination
Specimen answers to accompany the Specimen Paper 75/6

Advanced level Economics, Paper 3

These specimen answers should not be regarded as model or ideal answers, but rather as the type of answers that one might expect from a better than average candidate, one who identifies the main issues in the various questions.

1.

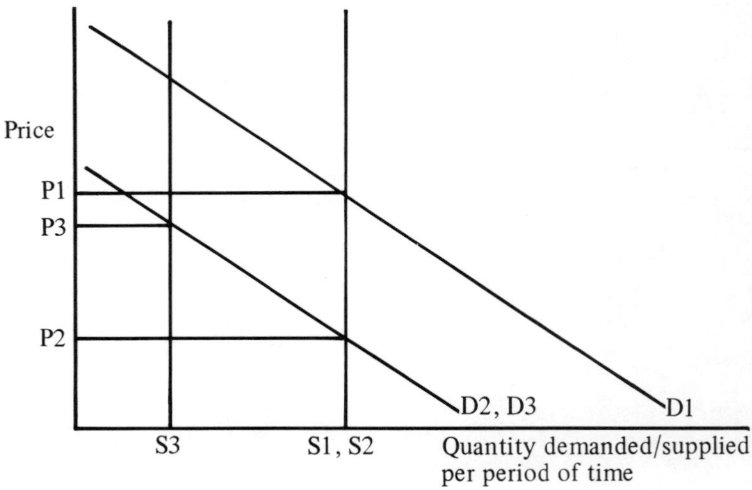

(a) The initial demand and supply curves are shown as D1 and S1, price being P1.
(b) Demand falls, the demand curve shifts to the left (D2) and the supply curve remains as before (S2). Price falls to P2.
(c) Supply falls, the supply curve shifts to the left (S3) and price rises again to P3. P3 might be equal to the initial price P1, or it might remain below this price, showing that farmers would be prepared to accept a slightly lower price than previously rather than undertake the additional costs required to send tomatoes to Fullbrook.

2. (a) The value of the multiplier is determined by the expression $\frac{1}{1 - MPC}$, We can see that domestic consumption at factor cost is 0·3 of income.

Therefore the multiplier is $\frac{1}{1-0.3} = \frac{1}{0.7} = 1.43$.

(b) There are three main leakages from the circular flow of income which reduce the value of the multiplier and which are identified in the table. These are:
Imports, which are 10(9 + 1), giving a propensity to import of 0.1;
Savings, which are 20(7 + 11 + 2), giving a propensity to save of 0.2; Taxation, which is 40(13 + 7 + 14 + 5 + 1), giving a propensity to tax of 0.4.
This shows that the most important single determinant of the value of the multiplier is taxation.

3. (a) The profit maximising output is that at which total revenue exceeds total cost by the greatest amount. We can see from the table that this is where the output equals eight units, profit being £49,000.

(b) (i) If additional fixed costs of £10,000 were incurred, the profit maximising output would remain unchanged, since the total cost is increased by the same amount, whatever the level of output. At eight units, profit would now be £39,000.

(ii) If additional fixed costs of £60,000 were incurred, there would now be no output at which total output exceeds total costs; i.e. a loss is made whatever the level of output. If the firm could foresee this situation it would go out of business rather than incur the additional fixed costs. If it could not foresee the situation it would continue in production in the short run, provided it could cover variable costs. Examining the situation at an output of eight units (which must still be the best position), we find that the situation is as follows:

Total cost:	£155,000
Fixed cost:	£75,000
Variable cost:	£80,000
Revenue:	£144,000

Therefore the firm will continue production in the short run but not in the long run.

4. Looking at the broad sectors which comprise the index of industrial production we see that, while output in manufacturing has increased, output has fallen in mining and quarrying. This fall in output is mainly due to a reduction in the demand for coal because of the increased competition from other fuels, especially oil.
Turning to manufacturing, we see that output has increased in most industries and this is what we would expect when the total population and national income were growing. There are only two industries in which output fell, shipbuilding and leather. The decline in shipbuilding is due to increased competition from other countries, e.g. Japan. The main reason for the decline in the leather industry was probably the decline in the production of shoes by British manufacturers. There might also have been a substitution of other materials, especially plastics for leather.
The biggest increases in output occurred in two groups of industries:
(i) Chemicals, and coal and petroleum products.
The changes in these industries result from a number of factors. Research and development work has increased the number of chemical products of various kinds: e.g. drugs, plastics, paints. Some of these products are derived from petroleum, which helps to account for the increase in output in this industry. On the demand side there have been large increases in the demand for drugs, for petrol, and for oil for use in central heating and the generation of electricity.
(ii) Engineering, especially instrument and electrical engineering.
Again, research and development work has led to a wider variety of machinery of various kinds, especially in the electronics field. This has meant that capital has been substituted for labour in many industries. Also important have been increased exports of British engineering products.
Most of the industries in the table make a wide variety of products whose output may change in very different ways. For example, we would expect to find that although food, drink and tobacco have grown at about an average rate

overall, the output of drink has grown at a much faster rate than the output of food, since it has a much higher income elasticity of demand.

5. These figures show clearly that in 1972 there were very wide differences in unemployment rates between different regions. The rate in the Development Areas was almost two-thirds above the average rate for Great Britain (which itself includes the Development Areas).
British governments have tried since 1945 to even out regional unemployment rates by means of various policies, and these figures seem to suggest that these policies have not been very successful. However, before we could come to a definite conclusion, we would require additional information on the following points:
   (i) The trend in regional unemployment rates over time. We cannot tell from one month's statistics whether the situation is improving or worsening.
   (ii) The number of new jobs created in the Development Areas as a result of government policies. Although unemployment is much heavier in the Development Areas than elsewhere, the difference might have been greater in the absence of government regional policies.
   (iii) The cost of creating new jobs in the Development Areas. The government often has to provide financial incentives to companies to move to Development Areas, and this expenditure could have been used for other purposes.
   (iv) The number of vacant jobs in the Development Areas. If it was found that there were large numbers of vacant jobs in the Development Areas, this would suggest that the unemployment was partly due to the unwillingness or the inability of these people to fill those jobs. This might be something that the government would find difficult to overcome except, perhaps, by more extensive training programmes.

APPENDIX II

THE SYLLABUS

Most A level examinations in Economics consist of two papers: an Objective Test paper (1½ hours) and a written paper (3 hours).
Reproduced below (by kind permission of the examining boards concerned) are three A level syllabuses in Economics.

UNIVERSITY OF CAMBRIDGE LOCAL EXAMINATIONS SYNDICATE

The multiple choice paper carries one third of the marks; the essay paper two-thirds of the marks. In the essay paper, candidates will be required to answer five questions, one of which must be chosen from a number of questions designed to test candidates' ability to interpret simple basic statistical data describing some important sector of contemporary economic activity in the U.K.

1. **The Central Problem of Economic Societies.** Scarcity, choice and allocation of resources; the market mechanism and planning.

2. **Theory of Demand.** Consumer behaviour; the derivation of individual and market demand curves; price, income and cross elasticities of demand. Total and marginal utility; joint demand; shifts in the demand schedule.

3. **Theory of Supply.** Behaviour of firms; the derivations of firm and industry supply curves; elasticity of supply. The short run; the law of variable proportions. The long run; economics and diseconomies of scale. Total, average and marginal costs.

4. **Price and Output Determination.** The interaction of supply and demand; price and output determination in different market structures; perfect competition, imperfect competition, monopoly. Total average and marginal revenues. Equilibrium of the firm and the industry in the short and long run.

5. **Theory of Distribution.** Demand for and supply of factors of production. The determination of wages, interest, profits and rent.

6. National Income Accounting. The definition and measurement of income, expenditure and output; net and gross; national and domestic; market prices and factor cost. Relationship between measures. Problems of comparison over time and between countries.

7. Theory of Income Determination. The circular flow of income: injections into the flow (investment, government expenditure, exports) and withdrawals from it (savings, taxes, imports). The consumption function. The multiplier. The equilibrium level of income. Inflationary and deflationary gaps.

8. Money and Prices. The nature and functions of money and credit. The demand for and supply of money. Definition and measurement of changes in the value of money. The money market: functions of the Bank of England, commercial banks and discount houses. Relationship between the Bank of England and commercial banks: reserve ratios. The operation of monetary policy: interest rates, open market operations, special deposits. The long term capital market and the finance of industry and trade. Causes and effects of changes in the price level.

9. International Trade. The gains from trade. The principle of comparative costs. Free trade and protection. Customs unions and free trade areas. Fixed and flexible exchange rates. The International Monetary Fund and present international monetary arrangements. The terms of trade. The United Kingdom balance of payments: current account (visible and invisible trade); currency flow and official financing.

10. The Role of the Government. Public provision and distribution of goods and services, e.g. education, housing, health, roads. The distinction between private and social costs. The management of national, regional and local economies. Policy instruments for influencing the rate of growth of output, the level of employment, the price level, the distribution of income and the balance of payments. Direct controls, fiscal and monetary policies, the regulation of prices and incomes. Measures to influence the location of industry and the distribution of employment, the regulation of monopolies and restrictive practices. The management of nationalised industries.

An understanding of economic principles is expected together with the ability to apply these principles to current problems. Candidates are expected to have a knowledge of the main economic institutions and problems of the United Kingdom and to be able to discuss government policy in relation to these.

Candidates are expected to be prepared for a simple quantitative approach to economic questions and should be able to calculate simple examples of: determination of price; elasticity of supply and demand; retail price index; terms of trade; exchange rates; national income; the multiplier; the accelerator. It is also expected that candidates will be able to interpret economic data in the form of tables, graphs and diagrams in relation to population, production, employment, earnings, growth, government income and expenditure, balance of payments and trade. Graphs and diagrams are expected to indicate meaning and to be clearly labelled.

Production

Specialisation and exchange. The concept of cost. Organisation of industry. Private and public sectors. Economies and diseconomies of scale. Consumption goods and capital goods. Location of industry.

Price

Function of the price mechanism in a free market. Centrally planned economies. Demand and supply. Price, income and cross elasticity. Price determination in perfect and monopoly markets. Elementary knowledge of other forms of imperfect competition including price discrimination. Long and short term applications.

Distribution

Rewards to the factors of production and the allocation of resources. The nature of rent, wages, interest and profit. Trade Unions, professional organisations and employers' organisations.

Population

Geographical and occupational distribution of the United Kingdom. Mobility of labour; economic effects of changes in size or distribution of population; emigration and immigration. Outline of world population problems.

Money and Financial Institutions

Nature and functions of money. The value of money and its measurement. Inflation and deflation. Savings Investment. Use of credit. Role of insurance companies and building societies. Hire-purchase. The British banking system. The Bank of England; the commercial banks, the money market; the capital market, merchant banking, the foreign exchange market. International monetary agencies.

International Trade

Theory of comparative costs. Tariffs and other restrictions on free trade. General Agreement on Tariffs and Trade. European Economic Community; European Free Trade Association. Standards of living and levels of productivity. Terms of trade. Balance of Payments. Capital movements. Exchange rates. International liquidity.

National Income and Expenditure

National Income, its measurement, and flow of money income between households, firms and the government. Aggregate supply and demand. Savings and investment. The multiplier and the accelerator. Productivity. Full employment. Prices and Incomes Policy. Economic growth. Economic indicators.

Public Finance

The Budget. Main sources of central government income and types of expenditure. The National Debt. Redistribution of income. The main sources of local government income and types of expenditure. Public corporation finance. Monetary and fiscal policy.

UNIVERSITY OF LONDON

Both papers carry equal weighting. The essay paper will be divided into two sections broadly corresponding to Section A and Section B of the syllabus, and candidates will be expected to answer questions from both sections.

Section A

The basic economic problem of scarcity and choice, and the significance of opportunity costs. The functions of the price system.

The relative inportance of the main industries and services (including agriculture) as contributors to the National Product, as employers of labour and as providers of exports and consumers of imports.

The role of markets and of firms. Forms of business organisation, including Co-operative Societies and nationalised industries. Exchange and specialisation (including international specialisation). The principle of comparative costs. Internal and external economies. The location of industry; concentration and diversification. Factors affecting the size of firms: vertical and horizontal integration.

Demand and supply analysis of prices in goods markets and factor markets, and the application of elementary price theory, e.g. price instability and the stabilisation of primary product prices, minimum and maximum price controls.

Changes in the size and composition of the population: its occupational and geographical distribution. Mobility of labour. The institutions of the labour market, e.g. Trade Unions and the services of the Department of Employment and Productivity.

The introductory treatment of market forms (perfect competition and monopoly). The causes of monopoly. Monopoly and public policy.

Section B
The level of money national income and the flow of money income between households, firms and the government. The elementary treatment of aggregate demand and supply in relation to changes in the general level of prices, output and employment, and the effects of government economic policy.

Nature and functions of money. Price indices. The role of a Central Bank and the commercial banks. The capital market and the finance of industry and trade.

The composition and elementary theory of the balance of payments. The terms of trade. Changes in the external value of currencies. International economic organisations. Elementary treatment of arguments for tariffs, e.g. protection against low-wage imports, the employment argument.

Government expenditure and the main sources of its revenue. The effect of taxes and subsidies, including the redistribution of income.

The growth of the real National Product and the broad determinants of real income per head.

SUGGESTED READING LIST

Economics in the Modern World by T. A. C. Shafto and W. R. Cook (Nelson)
Economics by P. A. Samuelson (McGraw – Hill)
Economics Theory by J. C. Powicke (Arnold)
A Texbook of Economics by J. L. Hanson (Macdonald & Evans)
An Introduction to Positive Economics by R. G. Lipsey (Weidenfeld & Nicholson)
Economics by F. Liversey (Polytech Publishers)
The Science of Wealth by C. F. Carter (Arnold)
An Introduction to Economic Behaviour by C. D. Harbury (Fontana)
Demand and Supply by R. Turvey (Allen & Unwin)

Candidates should be familiar with the main statistical series relating to the UK economy as published annually by H.M.S.O. e.g. **Annual Abstract of Statistics, National Income and Expenditure** and **Social Trends** (latest edition necessary in each case), together with **Facts in Focus** (Penguin).

A useful commentary on recent events is A. R. Prest and D. J. Coppock (editors): **The UK Economy: A Manual of Applied Economics** (latest edition) (Beekman Publications).

The Department of Employment issues a free monthly publication, **DE News**, which is obtainable from DE News, Department of Employment (Int. 3), 12 St. James Square, SW1Y 4LL.

The Information Division of the Treasury prepare a monthly report, **Economics Progress Report** which is obtainable free of charge from Circulation Section (H), Central office of Information, Hercules Road, London, SE1 7DU. **Treasury Broadsheets** are also obtainable free of charge from the Circulation and Promotion Section (TBS), Publications and Design Service Division of the Central Office of Information. A letter to the Distribution Unit, Reference Division of the Central Office of Information will enable you to obtain a sales list of reference documents many of which are excellent for students of Advanced Level Economics and all of which are priced very moderately.

CELTIC REVISION AIDS

An extensive range of study and revision material which may be used by students while preparing for a wide range of examinations. The material is designed such that the student can use it on his own and requires no supervision or guidance. It can be used equally well in a classroom or in the student's own home. The material can be used as part of a programmed revision course or as a last minute 'brush-up' on essential facts and examination techniques.

Series available are:

Model Answers A series aimed at GCE O Level, CSE, RSA and 16+ level examinations. Typical examination questions are presented and suggested answers are given. This series helps the student to remember essential facts and the best methods of presenting them in examination conditions.

Subjects covered in this series are: Julius Caesar, Macbeth, Romeo and Juliet, The Merchant of Venice, Essay Writing, Precis Writing, Mathematics, Physics, Chemistry, Biology, Human Biology, Commerce, Economics, and British Isles Geography.

Worked Examples A series with the same basis as the Model Answer series, but aimed at the GCE A Level and similar examinations. Subjects covered in this series are: Pure Mathematics, Applied Mathematics, Chemistry, Physics, Biology, Economics, Sociology, British History, and European History.

Multiple Choice O Level Multiple choice questions are a very important part of the examination requirements for GCE O Level and CSE. This series provides batteries of common questions and is also a very good way of revising essential facts. Subjects covered in this series are: English, French, Mathematics, Modern Mathematics, Chemistry, Physics, Biology, Human Biology, Commerce, Economics, and British Isles Geography.

Multiple Choice A Level Objective tests are now an important part of most A Level examinations. This series presents batteries of common questions and is also an excellent way of revising essential facts. Subjects covered in this series are: Pure Mathematics, Applied Mathematics, Chemistry, Physics, and Biology.
Test Yourself A series of pocket books designed for the revision of essential facts whenever the student has a free moment. Subjects covered in this series are: English Language, French, German, Commerce, Economics, Mathematics, Modern Mathematics, Chemistry, Physics, Biology, and Human Biology.

Celtic Revision Aids can make the difference between passing or failing your examinations.